005.54
JACOBS

WEST WYANDOTTE
KANSAS CITY KANSAS
PUBLIC LIBRARY
DATE:

APR - 6 2009

Excel® 2007 Charts

Made EASY

Kathy Jacobs
Curt Frye
Doug Frye

DISCARD

D1501861

McGraw Hill

New York Chicago San Francisco Lisbon
London Madrid Mexico City Milan New Delhi
San Juan Seoul Singapore Sydney Toronto

The *McGraw·Hill* Companies

Cataloging-in-Publication Data is on file with the Library of Congress

McGraw-Hill books are available at special quantity discounts to use as premiums and sales promotions, or for use in corporate training programs. To contact a special sales representative, please visit the Contact Us page at www.mhprofessional.com.

Excel® 2007 Charts Made Easy

Copyright © 2009 by The McGraw-Hill Companies. All rights reserved. Printed in the United States of America. Except as permitted under the Copyright Act of 1976, no part of this publication may be reproduced or distributed in any form or by any means, or stored in a database or retrieval system, without the prior written permission of publisher, with the exception that the program listings may be entered, stored, and executed in a computer system, but they may not be reproduced for publication.

1234567890   DOC DOC   0198

ISBN   978-0-07-160006-4
MHID   0-07-160006-X

Sponsoring Editor	**Acquisitions Coordinator**	**Indexer**	**Illustration**
Roger Stewart	Carly Stapleton	Karin Arrigoni	International Typesetting
Editorial Supervisor	**Technical Editor**	**Production Supervisor**	and Composition
Patty Mon	Jennifer Kettell	Jean Bodeaux	**Art Director, Cover**
Project Manager	**Copy Editor**	**Composition**	Jeff Weeks
Vastavikta Sharma,	Lisa McCoy	International Typesetting	**Cover Designer**
International Typesetting	**Proofreader**	and Composition	Jeff Weeks
and Composition	Paul Tyler		

Information has been obtained by McGraw-Hill from sources believed to be reliable. However, because of the possibility of human or mechanical error by our sources, McGraw-Hill, or others, McGraw-Hill does not guarantee the accuracy, adequacy, or completeness of any information and is not responsible for any errors or omissions or the results obtained from the use of such information.

This book is dedicated to the men who made it happen: my husband Bruce, my agent Neil, and my co-authors Curt and Doug. Thanks for sticking with it!

—Kathy Jacobs

This book is dedicated to my wife, Virginia.

—Curt Frye

This book is dedicated to my wife, Debbie.

—Doug Frye

About the Authors

Kathy Jacobs, Microsoft MVP in OneNote and PowerPoint, has been using Office since its earliest days. She started out using Word for newsletters, letters, books, and other documents in the late 1980s. She added PowerPoint and Excel to her areas of expertise in the early 1990s, and even still has the slides from one she created in 1991. She has been an active beta tester for Office since the 2002 release, and has almost every version of Office that has been released.

Kathy specializes in helping people from all backgrounds and walks of life learn to use Office to make their lives easier. As a PowerPoint and OneNote consultant, trainer, and writer, she has written on Office topics for her own site (www.OnPPT.com), Office On-Line, LockerGnome, IndeZine, and the PowerPoint FAQ. She presents regularly on a variety of subjects at user groups around Arizona. She has written three books: *Kathy Jacobs on PowerPoint* (Holy Macro! Books, 2004), *Unleash the Power of OneNote* (co-author) (Holy Macro! Books, 2004), and *Excel 2007: The L Line* (Wiley, 2007). She is the creator of Keystone Learning's OneNote 2003 training DVD. Right now, she specializes in helping people solve their Office emergencies through her service, Call Kathy Solutions.

Curt Frye is a professional freelance writer, consultant, and Microsoft Office Excel MVP. He has written sixteen books as sole author, most recently *Microsoft Office Excel 2007 Step by Step* (Microsoft Press, 2007) and the *Excel 2007 Pocket Guide* (O'Reilly Media, Inc., 2007), and was lead or contributing author on nine more books. In addition to his writing and consulting, Curt is a keynote speaker and corporate entertainer. You can find Curt online at www.thatexcelguy.com and www.curtisfrye.com.

Douglas W. Frye, Ph.D. is a consultant and professional writer. As the principal consultant for Skilled Analytics, L.L.C., Doug assists his clients in ensuring large-scale enterprise resource planning initiatives meet government requirements. In particular, Doug helps his clients establish how their project contributes to enterprise-wide integration, especially in the emerging service-oriented (Net-centric) arena. Doug is also an experienced academic and professional researcher. He is the author of *Network Security Policies and Procedures* (Springer, 2006), *Write Right Now!: Finishing Your Book After the Library's Closed* (Skilled Analytics L.L.C., 2008), and another book for the popular media, and has numerous papers and book chapters to his credit.

Contents at a Glance

Acknowledgments

Doug would like to acknowledge those who helped make this project a reality. Kathy Jacobs, as the principal author, and Dr. Neil Salkind of StudioB deserve great credit for taking an idea and presenting it in a way that made it a real project. Thanks also go to Roger Stewart of McGraw-Hill for his project leadership. Carly Stapleton of McGraw-Hill was unfailing in her professionalism and enthusiasm as I worked through drafting and revising my part of the book. Jennifer Kettell provided insightful feedback as technical editor and Lisa McCoy was great in helping me refine the text. Finally, I would like to thank my twin brother, Curt, for his advice and assistance, which aided me greatly in completing this project.

Introduction

Most people think of rows and columns of data when they think of Excel. In fact, when many think of Excel, they think of Mark Twain's saying "Lies, damned lies, and statistics." As users of Excel charting, the authors want to make sure that your data doesn't fall into the "damned lies" category. We want you to be able to tell the story from your data in ways that everyone can understand.

Excel 2007 Charts Made Easy is meant to change how you think about the data and the stories that data tells. In this book, we are going to help you learn not just how to make your charts, but also which charts to make.

The authors have drawn on their experience to create scenarios that you would find in the real world. Many of these scenarios are based on things the authors have encountered during their years of working with Excel. We have used these scenarios to help you determine which charts you will want to use with your data. But we know that the data alone won't help you understand Excel charts.

In order to truly understand how data fits into the different types of charts, we feel that you need to see the data and the charts built from it. So each chapter contains sample data and sample charts. You can find the actual Excel files on the web site associated with this book (www.mhprofessional.com). Use the sample files to help you learn more about how to make your charts amazing.

Excel 2007 Charts Made Easy is not made for you to read straight through, although you can. When you need to create a chart and aren't quite sure which one will fit your data best, pick up this book and use it to help you figure out what chart to create. When you need to expand your understanding of something in the charting world, pick up this book. When you know that there is a way to change that little piece that doesn't look right, pick up this book.

Our goal with this book is to help you become better at creating visual depictions of your data. People retain information better when they understand what they are looking at. Use the tips and ideas in this book to help people looking at your data better understand what you are showing them.
There are several pieces you will find in each chapter of the book:

- Memo sidebars make your life with Excel easier. Some are warnings about things you should never do. Others provide a different way to look at what you are doing. Some even provide hints about how to make an unwieldy chart behave the way you want it to.

- The Easy Way sidebars point out alternative ways to do things. Like all applications, there are many ways to do anything. Where there is an easier way, or where there is a quicker way, we have tried to point that out to you. The long way is still included in the chapter so that you understand what is going on behind the scenes.

- Briefings are found in the early chapters to help you understand the language of charting. These notes are intended to guide you through the language of charting. Each briefing contains a labeled chart and the definitions for the terms used on that chart. If you see a term used in a chapter that isn't clear to you, check the briefings earlier on in the book. Chances are the term is defined there.

Creating and Formatting a Basic Column Chart

When you open Excel 2007, you are faced with a spreadsheet made up of cells. Each cell contains either a piece of data or a formula that computes a piece of data. At the most basic level, that data is what Excel is all about.

However, pieces of data don't stand alone in this world. When you need to explain the data and what it means to someone else, showing them your glorious spreadsheet doesn't go very far. As the saying goes, "A picture says a thousand words." In the case of Excel, charts are the pictures.

Charts allow you to tell the story behind the data. They allow you to show the relationships between each piece of data. They can tell you the history of the data. They can even help you make decisions based on what the data has been so far and what it is projected to be in the future. But if your charts aren't clear and understandable, they will tell a more confusing story than just looking at the data would.

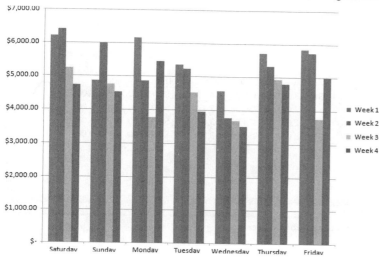

The most basic of charts in Excel is the column chart. The column chart is so common it is the first chart listed in the Insert | Charts group of Excel 2007. When you create a column chart, the data in the cells are grouped by the columns they are in. You can change the grouping, but the default is by column.

Column charts are good for showing how pieces of data collected over a range of categories are related to each other. The data might be amount of sales over time; it might be numbers of samples provided by type of store; it might be numbers of animals handled by a variety of veterinarians. In all column charts, there are sets of data that need to be compared.

Creating the Chart from Data

The first step in creating any chart is to determine what data you are going to chart. Let's start with a range of data that would be better shown as a column chart than in a table, as in Figure 1-1.

This spreadsheet shows the total sales for each day over four weeks. However, trying to figure out which days were good days and which were slow days isn't obvious. On the other hand, a glance at Figure 1-2 shows that Wednesdays are always the slowest sales days.

	A	B	C	D	E	F	G	H	I
1									
2	Day	Saturday	Sunday	Monday	Tuesday	Wednesday	Thursday	Friday	
3	Week 1	$6,200.00	$4,866.00	$6,148.00	$5,355.00	$4,564.00	$5,718.00	$5,838.00	
4	Week 2	$6,411.00	$5,982.00	$4,857.00	$5,236.00	$3,770.00	$5,334.00	$5,728.00	
5	Week 3	$5,237.00	$4,756.00	$3,771.00	$4,524.00	$3,684.00	$4,937.00	$3,763.00	
6	Week 4	$4,728.00	$4,520.00	$5,458.00	$3,955.00	$3,516.00	$4,799.00	$5,009.00	
7									
8									
9									
10									

My Chart / **Sheet1** / Sheet2 / Sheet3

Figure 1-1   Data table – total sales per day for four weeks

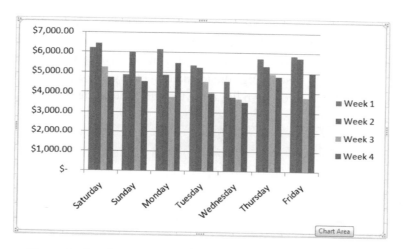

Figure 1-2   Data table – total sales per day for four weeks

To create the chart, you start by selecting the data to chart. Once you have the data selected, create the chart using Insert | Column. From the column charts available, select the chart type you want to use. Select the first option, a 2-D chart where the columns are clustered together.

Did you notice that when the chart was created, the available tabs in Excel changed? When you are working with *any* chart, you will get three new tabs: the Design, Layout, and Format tabs.

Use the Chart Tools | Design tab, shown in Figure 1-3, to work with the basic colors and design of the chart. The buttons on this tab enable you to change the type of the chart, what is shown in the chart, the colors of the chart, and basic layout of the chart.

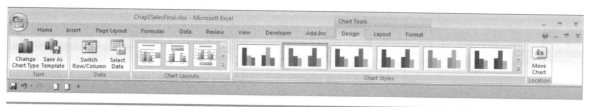

Figure 1-3   The Chart Tools | Design tab

Use the Chart Tools | Layout tab, shown in Figure 1-4, to do detailed formatting to either the entire chart area or any piece of the chart. You can turn on and off the parts of the chart (gridlines, walls, legend, etc.). You can also change the formatting of any part of the chart by selecting it from the dropdown list at the far right side of the ribbon.

Figure 1-4   The Chart Tools | Layout tab

Use the Chart Tools | Format tab, shown in Figure 1-5, to format the fills, lines, and effects for the chart, as well as the look and feel of any text in the chart.

Figure 1-5   The Chart Tools | Format tab

The buttons on these tabs are what allow you to turn your basic chart into something that will do a much better job of showing off your data. The chart created by Excel is not nearly as nice-looking or descriptive as you might like it to be. With a few quick clicks, you can improve not only the looks of the chart, but also how clearly the data tells its story.

THE LANGUAGE OF CHARTING

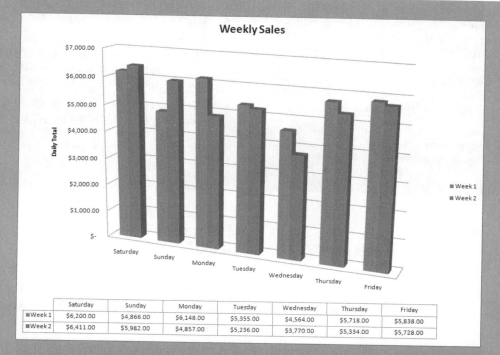

	Saturday	Sunday	Monday	Tuesday	Wednesday	Thursday	Friday
■Week 1	$6,200.00	$4,866.00	$6,148.00	$5,355.00	$4,564.00	$5,718.00	$5,838.00
■Week 2	$6,411.00	$5,982.00	$4,857.00	$5,236.00	$3,770.00	$5,334.00	$5,728.00

Charts have a language all their own. They use terms that are common in the rest of the world, but they have their own specific meanings in the Excel charting world:

- **Data or data points**   The information shown by the chart. In a column chart, the data is represented by columns of data running from the floor, or lowest value in the chart, to the maximum value.

- **Axis**   The dimensions for mapping the data. In a two-dimensional chart, they are x and y. Three-dimensional charts add a z axis as well.

- **Floor**   The bottom of the chart. On a two-dimensional chart, the floor is just a line. On a three-dimensional chart, it is like the floor of the box that contains the chart.

- **Columns**   The representation of the data. This might be counts of items, dollars spent, cases closed, or almost anything else.

- **Values**   Running up one side of the chart are the values that the bars represent. In this example, the values are dollars, but they might be gallons or nearly anything else.

THE LANGUAGE OF CHARTING (CONT.)

- **Series**   The groups of data being charted. In this example, each week is a series. If the chart had just shown the values for each date, with no grouping, there would be only one series in the chart. Series are usually shown in a chart by using a common color or other fill for the bars related to that series.

- **Gridlines**   The lines on the background of the chart that help indicate what value the column represents. Gridlines can run horizontally, vertically, or both.

- **Legend**   The map showing which color or fill represents which series.

- **Title**   The heading at the top of the chart. This is the descriptive text that tells the story you want the audience to learn from the chart.

- **Data sheet grid**   The actual data used to create the chart. This is not usually shown, but can be helpful if the differences between the data points don't show well on the chart.

Making It Clearer

The clarity of your chart isn't just related to the clarity of your data. It also has to do with making it easy for someone looking at the data to draw conclusions from the data. As with many things in life, how you present your data will help people see what you want them to see.

No matter what kind of chart you are creating, one of the easiest things you can do to make it clearer is to make it bigger. You could grab one of the corners of the chart and expand it. This would leave the chart on the same page as the data. At first glance, that seems to be a good idea. However... if you leave your chart on the same page as the data, there is a good chance that it will cover up your data and get in the way when you are working with it. Charts on the same page as data are also easy to accidentally delete. I recommend...

The next step is to turn on the legend. One way to do this is to use the Chart Tools | Layout | Legend button. This button lets you select where you want the legend to show on your chart. To activate your legend, click the button and select from the drop-down list. You can also add the legend by choosing a chart layout (which will be covered at the end of this chapter) or by using More Legend Options, which will be covered in Chapter 2.

THE EASY WAY

With the chart selected, find and click the Chart Tools | Design | Move Chart button. Select the New Sheet option, and give the new sheet a descriptive name. Click OK. A new sheet will be added to your Excel file. This sheet will contain the chart and only the chart. By placing your chart on its own page, you ensure that the chart won't be accidentally deleted by a mis-click while you are working with your data. In addition, by placing it on its own sheet in the file, the chart itself will be bigger and more readable.

The third step in improving your chart is to decide if the data is grouped the way you want it to be. Any data in a column chart can be grouped by rows or columns. By default, Excel groups your data by rows. This means that the data was grouped by weeks, with each week containing seven bars. If you want to know which of the weeks have the best and worst sales, you could tell it from this chart. However, if you want to know which were the best and worst days, you need to make a change.

Click the Chart Tools | Design | Switch Rows/Columns button. Notice that the grouping of the data swaps from weeks to days. Now you can tell at a glance that Saturdays are the best days and Wednesdays are the worst days. Changing the grouping of your data can sometimes tell you things you didn't know the data had to say.

X, Y, Z – Axis to Axis

The column chart in this chapter has been created as a two-dimensional chart. You might think about this as being drawn on a wall of a room. It is flat. The x axis is the line between the floor of the room and the wall itself. The y axis is the line between the wall and the one to its right. The higher the value for a column, the taller it is on the wall. The more columns you have, the narrower each is, since they all have to fit on the same wall.

But this isn't all there is to a column chart. You can create a third axis. You might think of this as moving the chart from the wall to the middle of the room. The bottom of the chart then becomes the entire floor instead of just a line. This isn't just changing the shapes in the chart to have depth and edges. This is adding depth to the chart by adding a third axis to the chart: the z axis.

The third axis isn't just an axis where data is plotted. It is a change to how the chart looks and how the data in it is perceived. One of the advantages to having the third axis is that you are no longer restricted to looking at the chart face-on. You can change your view of the chart so that you can see it from above, below, or any side.

To see how the third axis changes your chart, click Chart Tools | Design | Change Chart Type. The list of available charts will show up. For now, pick

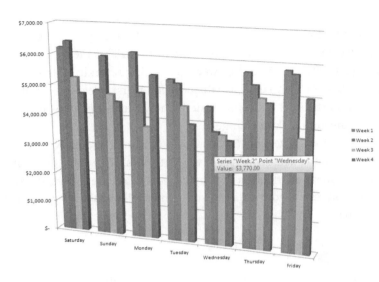

3-D Clustered Columns (the fourth chart in the list of column charts). The chart appears to angle away from you, looking much like Figure 1-6.

Adding a third dimension isn't always a great idea. When you add the ability to see a chart from above or from the side, you also add the ability for bars to get in each other's way. This is more obvious with the regular 3-D column chart than with the clustered one, as shown in Figure 1-7.

Figure 1-6   3-D clustered columns chart

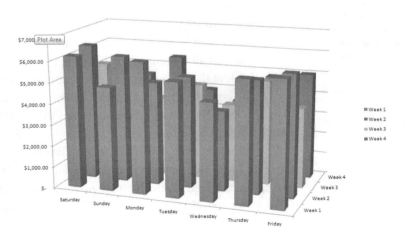

Figure 1-7   Regular 3-D column chart

In this chart, higher columns make it hard to see the columns behind them. One way you can fix this is by making some of the columns transparent so that the others show through. This will work with some charts, but not with others.

Making Chart Objects Transparent

To make your chart columns transparent, you are going to need to select the series you want to change and format it. You are likely to find that you need to do this with more than one series. To make it easier to select things, use Chart Tools | Layout | Current Selection to select the first series to be made transparent. Either click the Format selection button or right-click the series and select Format Data Series. On the Fill page, change the fill to Solid and slide the transparency slider to the right. Watch the fill on the shape as you do. You want the shape to still have some color and substance, but not block the columns behind it. Twenty-five percent is usually a good number for this front series.

When you are working with the various format dialogs in Excel 2007, the changes are applied as soon as you make them. If you want to reformat something else, just change the selection, and the dialog will follow along. To see this, change the selection from Series "Week 1" to Series "Week 2." On the Fill page, change the fill to Solid. Notice that this time, the color of the series changed. Change it back to a reddish color, and then change its transparency. Change the transparency for any of the columns that are hiding other columns, and your chart will look approximately as shown in Figure 1-8.

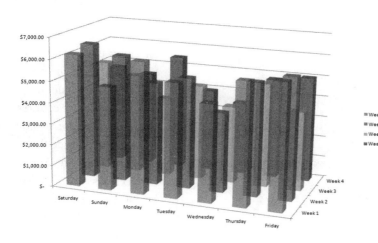

Figure 1-8 Reformatted 3-D chart with transparent columns

9

MEMO

Some people find the transparency tools confusing, since they seem to be set up backwards. One hundred percent transparent means that the object is totally invisible and will not show at all. You seldom want this in a chart. Settings in the 40 to 55 percent range tend to allow for the objects behind to be seen, while still giving body to the object being formatted.

THE EASY WAY

Want to quickly remove the transparency from your columns? You can do it quickly from the context menu. Right-click the first set of columns in the chart, and select Reset to Match Style. Repeat this for each area you have formatted, and your chart will be back to its original state.

Do you notice a problem? Even making the columns transparent doesn't let you see some of the Week 4 and Week 5 columns. This is because the objects are not really drawn on the chart when the chart is rendered at this angle. You might think of them as being so totally behind the other columns in the room that you can't get a view of them from the current angle.

In this case, you need to change the viewing angle for the chart—you need to move around in the room so that the full set of data is able to be seen.

Turning a 3-D Chart Around

The easiest way to turn your chart is to use the Chart Tools | Layout | 3-D Rotation button. When you click this button, you get the Format Chart Area dialog with the 3-D Rotation options selected, as shown in Figure 1-9.

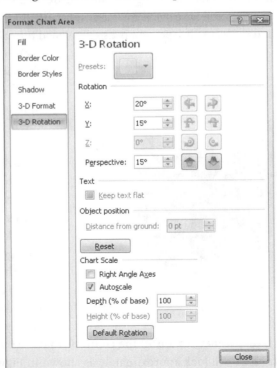

Using the values and arrows on this dialog, you can adjust the rotation about each of the three axes of your chart. Think of this as a way to move around the chart. Use the arrows or values to the right of the X value to rotate the chart clockwise or counter-clockwise. Use the Y values and arrows to rotate the chart up and down. For some charts, you will also be able to rotate the chart around its middle axis. (In this chart, you can't.)

Figure 1-9   Format Chart Area dialog

MEMO

If you need to move where the legend is, click it while the Format dialog is open. The options shown will change to the Legend Options list, and you can use the options to change where you want the legend in relation to the chart.

For this chart, if you change the X value to 130, you will find that you are looking at the back of the chart instead of the front. Because these numbers are lower, you can see all of the columns from this view. In addition, if you change the Y value to 30 (so that the chart is tipped slightly towards you), the columns and their values become even more distinct, as shown in Figure 1-10.

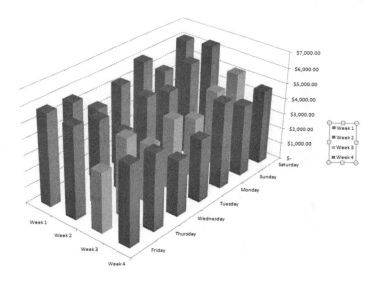

Figure 1-10   Rotated chart

BAR CHARTS VS. COLUMN CHARTS

When you look at the chart types you can insert and create from Excel 2007, you may notice that there are column charts and bar charts. There really isn't much difference between the two. The biggest difference is that column charts run the data bars vertically and bar charts run the data bars horizontally. Another difference is that when you create a bar chart, you can only create clustered bars, not grouped bars.

The real difference between the two is visible in a chart option not yet covered: stacked charts. Stacked charts let you see all of the data for a single row in one bar. This allows you to see how things total up. Both of the charts shown in Figures 1-11 and 1-12 were created from the same data used in the other examples in this chapter.

The stacked column charts are useful if you are going to be looking at the overall totals. Because you

BAR CHARTS VS. COLUMN CHARTS (CONT.)

read right to left, your eye scans across the total lines fairly easily and finds the top of each bar. On the other hand, if you are looking to contrast how a day went across the weeks, you will find the stacked bar chart easier. Your eye will translate each segment of the bar as its own story and (again) connect the pieces as you gaze the bar.

Want to know more? Check out Chapter 2.

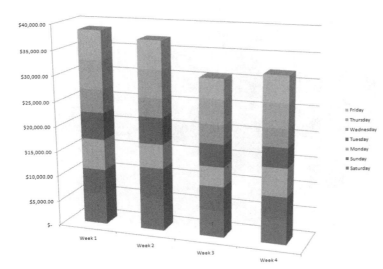

Another advantage to changing both the X and Y rotation is that the chart no longer overwrites the legend. Rotating the chart doesn't rotate the legend, so if you decide to only rotate around one axis, you will find that you need to move the legend as well. For some charts, you will also need to uncheck Right Angle Axes to get the look you want. Try it both ways and see which you prefer. The answer will depend on the chart itself.

Figure 1-11 Stacked column chart

Shapes and Your Chart

In addition to having the data in your chart represented by bars, you can have them represented by a number of other shapes. Select a data series, and bring up the Format dialog. Go to the Shape section, and you can see that there are four basic shapes you can choose from, as shown in Figure 1-13, specifically:

- **Boxes**   The bars you have seen so far in this chapter
- **Cylinders**   Bars with circular tops and bottoms

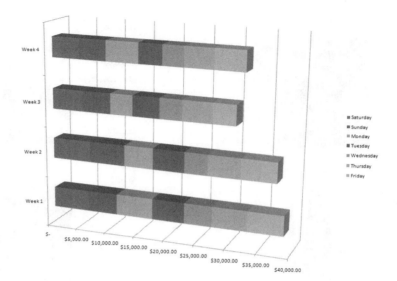

Figure 1-12   Stacked
bar chart

- **Cones**   Cylinders with circular bottoms that taper to a point at the top

- **Pyramids**   Bars with square bottoms that taper to a point at the top

Here is the data from Week 1 on four different charts. In each chart, the data is represented by a different shape. As you can tell, the choice between cylinders and bars is a personal preference thing. Cylinders look more modern, but the bars work for some data as well. You may prefer edged pieces, or you may prefer rounded pieces. Your choice in shape may also be influenced by the data you are representing. If your data is coins, you definitely want to use cylinders instead of columns. If your data is bricks, you want columns instead of cylinders. You will need to make the same choice when deciding between cones and pyramids. Cones and pyramids lend themselves to data where the top of the chart represents a diminishing item instead of a steady item. For example, if the chart was showing losses instead of sales, you might want to use the cones or pyramids to show the diminishing numbers.

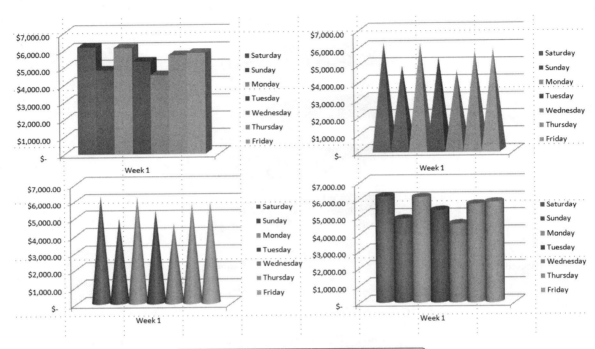

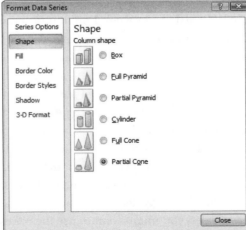

Figure 1-13   Four different shapes in graphs

Choosing pyramids or cones gives you an extra option: Full or Partial. By default, charts created with pyramids and cones are set to Full. When you change the bar shape to Partial, the shapes are adjusted to show the relationship between the current data element and the biggest data element. In order to make this more obvious, the example in Figure 1-14 is going to use slightly different data than that which has been used so far this chapter.

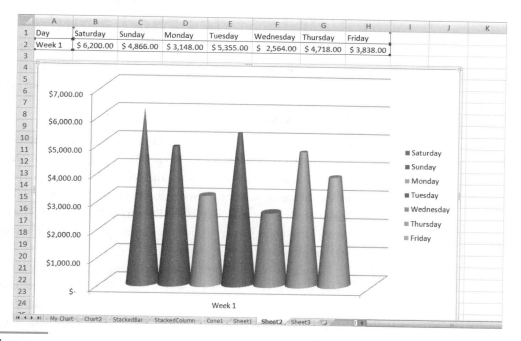

Figure 1-14   Partial cones chart

One advantage to the partial cones or pyramids is that you can see at a glance which data points are the low points on the graph. In this case, the cutoff cones make it clear that Mondays are bad sales days, but that Wednesdays are the worst day of the week.

There is one problem that can occur when using the partial shapes. Because the fullest shape comes to an exact point, it is sometimes hard to see what the actual value is for the largest data point. All of the other points come to flattened tops, but Saturday's data goes to a point—you need to look closely at it to see what the actual value for Saturday's sales was.

Formatting Your Chart with the Built-in Styles and Layouts

Instead of doing all the chart formatting and layout by hand, it is a good idea to start with the styles and layouts available with Excel 2007. The styles and layouts give you a head start to creating just what you need for your chart.

Chart Styles

Chart styles define the colors and effects used on your charts. They define what color will be used for each bar, whether the background is white or colored, whether the walls show, and what color the walls are. You are going to see the same basic chart styles for all charts, but there will be differences, based on whether the chart is a 2-D chart or a 3-D chart. The different chart styles for 2-D graphs are shown in Figure 1-15. The different chart styles for 3-D graphs are shown in Figure 1-16.

The chart styles are organized in columns. Each column is a different style, based on one of the color sets in the file. The first column is usually the grayscale choices. The second column is the "colorful" choice (meaning each bar is a different color). The other columns show the data all charted in the same basic color, with hues used to differentiate the data elements.

If you don't like the color choices provided in the styles list, you can change the colors by manually formatting the chart. For information on that, check out Chapter 2.

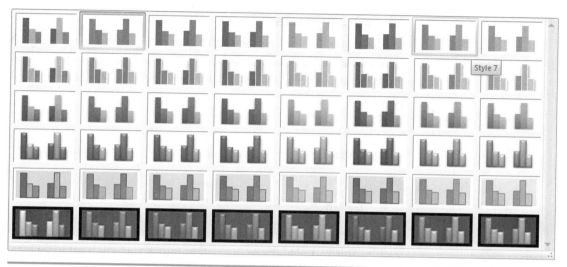

Figure 1-15   Chart styles for 2-D graphs

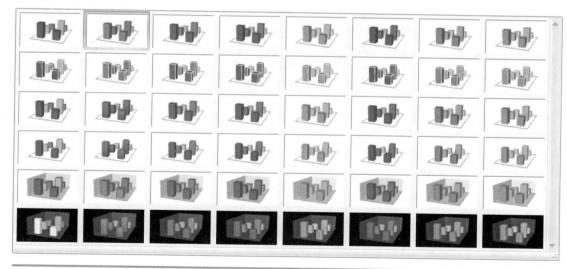

Figure 1-16   Chart styles for 3-D graphs

Chart Layouts

The layout for the first chart in this chapter is the default column chart layout. It shows the data itself in columns. The legend for the chart is shown to the right. The chart layout defines whether and where the following items are visible on your chart:

- Title

- Legend

- Values

- Datasheet

Unlike the first chart, the rest of the charts in this chapter have the title visible. This is probably one of the first things you will want to do for your charts. You can turn on the chart title by selecting Layout 1 from the Chart Tools | Design | Chart Layouts list. (Layouts 2, 3, 5, 6, 8, 9, and 10 also show the title.) Once you have a title placeholder showing, click in the text box, select the text, and replace it with the correct title for your chart.

There are a total of ten chart layouts defined. These layouts are helpfully named Layout 1 through Layout 10. Each layout is a different combination of the four extra items listed previously. Play around with the layouts on both 2-D and 3-D charts, as they apply differently to the two classes of column charts.

Creating and Formatting a Basic Bar Chart

If bar charts are column charts with the data bars running horizontally instead of vertically, why include a full chapter on them? Because this chapter covers formatting your bar charts by hand. While you can format your bar and column charts with the default formatting available in Excel 2007, you are quickly going to find that you need to make more detailed changes to your charts. While the default styles, formats, and setups for charts create nice-looking charts, you need to be able to target the look of your charts to match the materials you are creating with the charts.

The illustration at left is a good example of a chart that works better as a bar chart than as a column chart. This chart shows weight loss in pounds by the members of an eight-person team. In this case, the data is presented as a stacked bar chart. By stacking the data instead of making individual bars for each person's weekly loss, you not only see at a glance how much weight was lost, but also how much was lost each week.

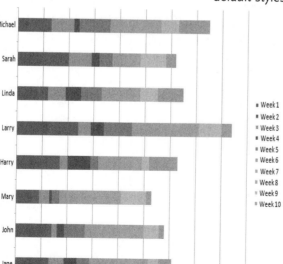

Another issue that comes up when creating charts is deciding what data to chart. With some charts, you will want to show the full set of data. With other charts, you will only want to show summary information. In this case, charting possibilities include the actual week-by-week losses, the total lost per person, the average lost per person, or the median lost per person. Depending on which of these you are charting, your chart will be formatted in different ways.

So why manually edit the formatting of charts? The tendency is to use the predefined formatting options. After all, it is easier. But since it is easier to use the default options, you run the risk of having your charts look like everyone else's. You want to make sure that the charts you create stand out from the crowd. You want people to remember what you have to tell them. At the same time, you don't want to take your style and formatting changes too far over the top—standing out because the chart looks hideous is usually worse than blending into the crowd.

Creating the Chart from Data

The first step in creating any chart is to determine what data you are going to chart. Figure 2-1 shows the data used to create the tables in this chapter.

	A	B	C	D	E	F	G	H	I	J
1	Person	Jane	John	Mary	Harry	Larry	Linda	Sarah	Michael	
2	Week 1	5	6	3	4.5	6	4	4.5	2	
3	Week 2	1.5	1	1.5	4	6	2	5.5	4.5	
4	Week 3	3	1	2	1.5	2.5	3.5	4.5	4.5	
5	Week 4	2.5	1.5	0.5	4.5	2.5	3	1.5	1	
6	Week 5	2.5	4	1.5	1.5	5.5	4	2.5	6	
7	Week 6	1.5	2	3.5	4.5	4.5	2.5	2	2.5	
8	Week 7	5	4.5	2.5	2	3	4	2.5	2.5	
9	Week 8	5	5	6	2	5.5	1	1	5	
10	Week 9	2	3	5	1.5	4.5	3.5	5	3.5	
11	Week 10	2.5	1	1	5.5	2	5	2	6	
12	Average w	3.05	2.9	2.65	3.15	4.2	3.25	3.1	3.75	
13	Maximum	5	6	6	5.5	6	5	5.5	6	
14	Median w	2.5	2.5	2.25	3	4.5	3.5	2.5	4	
15	Total lost	30.5	29	26.5	31.5	42	32.5	31	37.5	
16										

Figure 2-1   Data table – weight lost by week

MEMO

If you can't decide if your data should be displayed in clustered bars or stacked bars, use this simple rule: If you want to see at a glance the total of the data for each series, use a stacked bar. If you want to compare the data for each element in the series, use the grouped bars.

MEMO

Just be careful when you do manual formatting. Make sure that you don't go overboard and make your chart a conglomeration of colors and styles that get in the way of understanding the story behind the data. Unless, of course, you want to muddy the story of your data. In that case, go back to the beginning and decide what your charts say versus what they should say.

While individual people will want to see their numbers in a table, as in the figure, when you are showing progress or reporting results, the table doesn't get the point across as well as a chart would. Using a bar chart to show the results allows you to pull the viewer's eye across the page or the screen to show both the details and the overall results. Each piece of the bar tells a piece of the story, while the bars themselves show the total amount of weight each person lost.

Because this data contains rows of information other than just the weekly reporting data, you cannot create the chart from a single cell selection. If you create the chart with just a single cell selected, Excel 2007 will select all of the contiguous data and create a stacked bar chart from the table. In this case, the bars will then have one segment for each member of the team. In addition there will be bars for the average, maximum, and median values for each team member (see Figure 2-2). Even if the rows and columns are switched using Chart Tools | Design | Switch Rows/Columns, the chart still doesn't make much sense. Once the data is switched, the average, maximum, and median segments show at the end of the weight loss bar.

Instead, you need to drag to select the data you want to chart. If you want to chart the actual weight lost, select cells A1 to I11. Once the data is selected, click Insert | Bar and select Stacked Bar. The resulting graph shows the weight lost every week by the team. From this chart, you can see exactly how much weight was lost by whom in which week. If you want to see the weight loss by person instead of by week, switch the rows and columns. The result is the chart at the beginning of the chapter.

Formatting Chart Parts

While the easy way to format your chart is to use the default styles, your charts will stand out better if you learn how to tweak the default styles to improve the look of your charts. Any part of the chart that can be seen can be tweaked and improved.

THE LANGUAGE OF CHARTING

Charts have a language all their own. They use terms that are common in the rest of the world, but they have their own specific meanings in the Excel charting world. Most of the terms for bar charts apply equally to column charts.

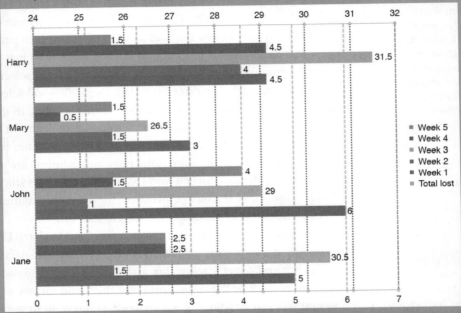

- **Stacked bar charts** A chart where a single bar/column of data is created for each series of data. Shows totals as well as the individual data elements.

- **Clustered bar charts** A chart where each data point is represented by an individual bar. Data points from the same series are grouped together. Groups of bars are also known as clusters of bars.

- **100% stack** A stack where the values for each element represent the part of the whole instead of the actual data.

- **Bar** Vertical representation of data.

- **Gap** The space between grouped or clustered bars.

- **Series overlap** The amount of space between series items in a group of bars. If the space is positive, the bars overlap. If it is negative, the bars have space between them.

- **Chart area** The background for the entire chart. When you select the chart area, you are working with an area that is variable in size. This is in contrast to the plot area.

THE LANGUAGE OF CHARTING (CONT.)

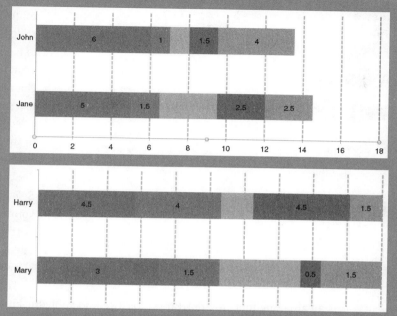

- ■ **Plot area** The area holding the chart itself. The size of this area will be set by the size of the chart. It is bounded by the axes. The plot area is always smaller than the chart area.

- ■ **Gridlines** The lines on the background of the chart that help indicate what value the column represents. Gridlines can run horizontally, vertically, or both.

- ■ **Primary axis** The axis with the values for the main data in the chart.

- ■ **Secondary axis** The axis with the values for secondary data in the chart. A secondary axis is used when the range of data values is too large to create an understandable chart.

Chart Area and Plot Area

The predefined backgrounds for your charts are either solid white or gray flowing to black. These are the defaults because they give your charts a nice, clean look. But sometimes, you will want to add a bit of dash to the chart background to help tell the story.

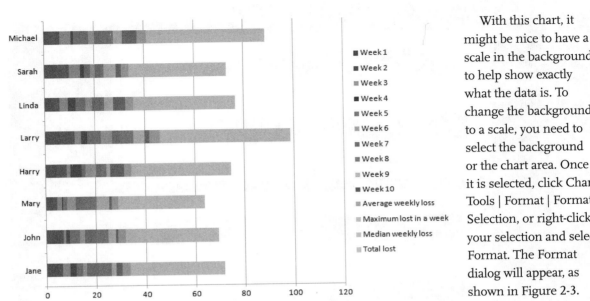

Figure 2-2   Stacked bar chart with the wrong data

With this chart, it might be nice to have a scale in the background to help show exactly what the data is. To change the background to a scale, you need to select the background or the chart area. Once it is selected, click Chart Tools | Format | Format Selection, or right-click your selection and select Format. The Format dialog will appear, as shown in Figure 2-3.

The Format dialog is an amazing tool. You don't need to close it to apply the changes you want to make. Make the change in the dialog box, and it will be applied to the selection immediately. This also means that if you want to format another item, you can select that item without closing the dialog. Test it out for yourself. It can be quite handy.

To change the background of the chart, click the option for the type of fill you want to use. Good choices for backgrounds are graphics that fade out, gradients that complement your data colors, or solid colors that complement your data colors. If you choose one of the white background styles, the background fill will be No Fill. If you choose one of the black background styles, the background fill is Automatic.

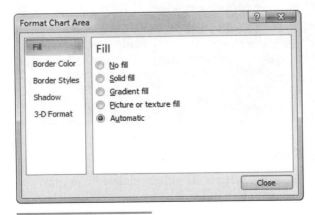

Figure 2-3   The Format dialog

THE EASY WAY

On both the Format and Layout tabs, there are a group of tools that will help you with your manual formatting: the Current Selection tools. If you use the drop-down box at the top of the group to select the items to format, you will always know exactly what you are working with. In addition, if you use the Format Selection button to bring up the Format dialog, you will never mis-select the content you want to format.

To make the background a picture of a scale, choose Picture or Texture Fill, and then click the Clip Art button. This will bring up the Select Picture dialog. This dialog lets you select from the pictures on your hard drive, on Office Online, or both. To search for a piece of clip art, type the search word in the box, and click Go. If you type the word **scale** as your search term, you should find a picture of a white bathroom scale. This picture is available from Office Online. Click that picture to select it, and click the Apply button to use it, as shown in Figure 2-4.

The chart area will change to the scale. The problem is that only the edges of the scale show. The next step is to change the plot area so that it is either transparent or has no fill. This will allow the background to show through.

Change the selection to the plot area. The current fill for it is probably Automatic. That tells Excel that the fill for the plot area should be picked up from whatever color scheme is in use. When the color scheme is changed,

THE EASY WAY

Like the look of the black background chart styles, but don't want them grey/black? That background effect is achieved by having the chart area black and the plot area grey. Start with the default set, and then format the two areas as you desire.

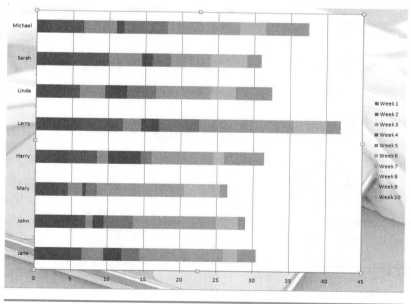

Figure 2-4   The chart with the scale as a background – first try

25

THE EASY WAY

Creating charts for print? If you have the ability to use color, use it. It will draw attention to your charts. If you don't, then use the chart styles in the first column of the styles gallery. These styles are specially designed to work with greyscale print.

the color will change. That would be great, except... You can't change the transparency of an automatic fill. In order to see the new background, you need to change either to a solid fill or to no fill. I prefer no fill in these cases, since it doesn't add extra work if I change color sets later.

With no fill for the plot area, the picture shows through. The problem is that it is dark enough to distract from the chart. Reselect the chart area, and use the slider at the bottom to set the transparency to about 50 percent. Now the graphic won't distract from the chart, but it still shows enough to give a hint of what the chart is about, as shown in Figure 2-5.

Try out the other settings for the chart and plot backgrounds. The more you experiment, the better you will learn what you like and don't like for backgrounds.

Bars

The most obvious formatting you can do with your bars is to make them look better by improving the fills. Because of the printing restrictions on this book, most of the charts here have been created using the multicolored styles. Since these are the styles many other users will pick first, try avoiding them for real-life use. Either use one of the toned color styles or create your own fills.

When you create your

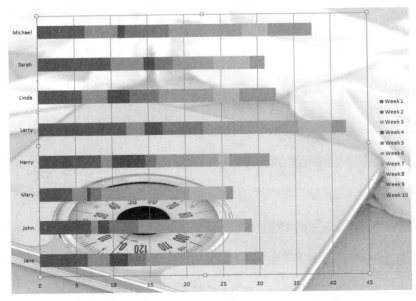

Figure 2-5 The chart with the scale as a background

own fills for the items in your charts, you ensure that the charts are going to be unique to what you are doing, the product you are reporting on, and the companies you create materials for. If you have predefined colors, use

MEMO

If you're using stacked bars, avoid using pictures for the fills. Each segment of the bar will be filled with an individual picture. This look can be jarring.

gradients to give your bars a bit of personality. If don't have predefined colors, use graphics to make your charts stand out. But before you go there....

To fill your bars with a gradient fill, first you need to select them. Once they are selected, bring up the Format dialog. Go to the Fill options. The current selection is probably Automatic. To use a gradient fill instead, click the options for a gradient. Each bar will fill with the default gradient. If you have not used a gradient fill in this file, the gradient will be gray to light gray, as shown in Figure 2-6. If you have previously set a gradient, that gradient will be used.

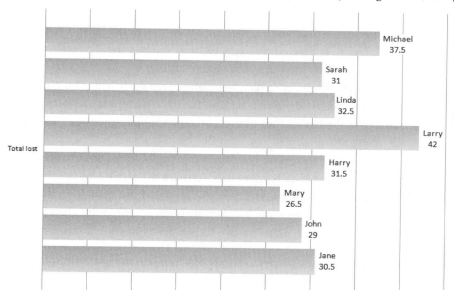

Gradients are created by defining the colors for each stop in the color flow and the distances between each stop. To change the gradient, select the stop, and then use the color drop-down list to pick the color for that stop. Continue choosing a color for each stop, and you will have a nice gradient fill for your bars.

Another great fill for your bars is a graphic

Figure 2-6 The chart with gradient bars

that represents your data. For this chart, using stacked copies of pictures of the individuals would work nicely and is easy to do. Your first step is to put an electronic copy of the individual's picture on your computer's hard drive. Ensure you have only the bar for the employee selected (not the full series of bars). On the list of fills, select Picture or Texture. Click Picture and navigate to the picture for your fill. By default, Excel is going to stretch your picture to fill the whole bar. This isn't what you want. Instead, choose Stack or Stack and Scale.

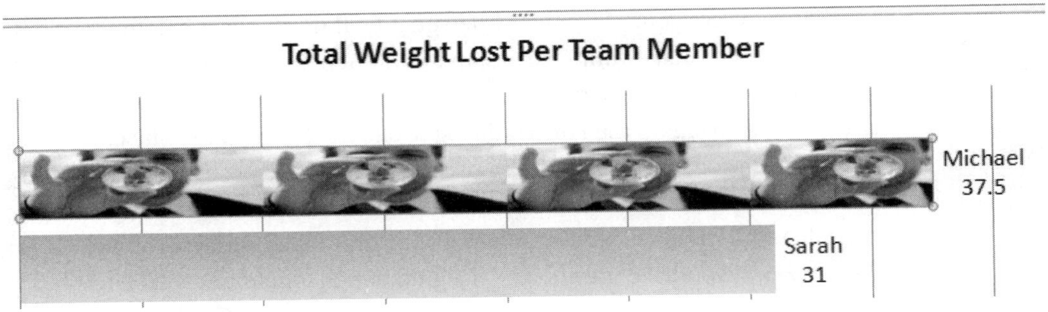

Total Weight Lost Per Team Member

Michael
37.5

Sarah
31

Figure 2-7   Michael's bar with picture fill stacked and scaled 1 to 10

Stack takes the picture and tiles it across the bar, as shown in Figure 2-7. Stack and Scale allows you to define how many pictures will be used. The scale equates to how many data points you want each picture to cover.

Play around with a variety of pictures. Some sizes work better for chart fills than others. It depends in part on how busy the picture is and how close it is to the size of the bar you are filling. If the picture has to be stretched or squashed, it will not work well as a bar fill.

Just as you can use the Format dialog to change the fill of your bars, you can also use it to change the borders used to mark the outer edges of the bars. When you format the borders, you will set two different values: the border color and the border style. Most of the border settings are clear and understandable. However, there are two things here you should watch out for:

- If you don't want a border around your bars, set the border color to No Line. I don't know why no line is a border color, but it is.

- What you set the border color to affects what choices you have for border styles. If you choose Automatic for the border color, changing the values on the border style list will set the border color to No Color. If you then choose a new border style, it will stay as No Line and ignore the style change. If you choose No Color for the border color, then choosing a value for any of the border styles will change the border color to a solid line. Note that choosing No Color has different results than having it revert to no color.

28

Axes and Grid Lines

Just as you can change the borders around the bars, you can also change the lines that make up the x and y axes and the grid lines. Select the item or items you wish to change and format their color, style, or shadow.

If you want to change the spacing for the gridlines, you need to use the Chart Tools | Layout | Gridlines gallery. Each bar chart has horizontal and vertical gridlines. For each of these two types of gridlines, you can show

- **No gridlines**

- **Major gridlines**   Just the gridlines for the units that show on the axis

- **Minor gridlines**   Just the gridlines for the individual units on the axis

- **Major and minor gridlines**   All gridlines for the axis are shown, but the major ones are darker than the minor ones

Once you set the gridlines you want to see, formatting the gridlines is done by activating the Format dialog for that set of gridlines. In addition to being able to choose the line color and style for the gridlines, you can add a shadow to the lines. Shadows can be nice things, but don't go overboard with them. If you are going to have both major and minor gridlines in both directions, you don't need to shadow the lines as well.

Once you know which gridlines you want to show, it is time to decide how many to show for each gridline. This is done by selecting one of the axes and bringing up the Format Axis dialog. Most of this dialog will look familiar by now. But there are two new sets of options to play with.

Axis Options, the first set in the list, defines how many tick marks (and, therefore, gridlines) will be on the chart. The tick-mark interval can be between 1 and 31,999. Once you know how many tick marks you are going to have for an axis, you can customize the interval between the marks, the type of axis, the location of the marks, and the cross points for the axis. Most of the time, you won't bother. Excel 2007's charting engine is pretty smart about deciding where to place the gridlines, labels, and tick marks. The only time you are likely to go in and mess with these items is if you need to change the location where the two axes cross. If you have negative values in your bar chart, you may find that you need to change the crossing location for the two axes.

The other new category of formatting options is the Alignment options. These options customize where the text labels are placed in relation to the current axis. You control the alignment of the text, the direction of the text, and the angle of the text.

Figure 2-8   Format Data Series tab – series options

Gaps

When creating charts with only one bar in a group, the default is to have the data spread along the chart in an evenly spaced manner. The space between the bars is the same width as the bars themselves. This is the gap between the bars. When creating charts with many bars in a group, the default gap between the groups is a little more than the width of a single bar. With clustered bars, there is a second type of gap to deal with—the gap between the bars in the group, called the series overlap.

Formatting of both the gap and the series overlap is done by selecting a series and formatting it. The first tab, Format Data Series, allows you to set both the overlap and the gap for this series, as shown in Figure 2-8.

The amount of gap between series can make a chart more readable or totally unreadable. If you have more data than easily fits on the chart, overlapping the series and minimizing the gap can increase how much data is on the chart. Going too far with the overlapping will hide some of the bars. Going too far with the gap will eliminate the demarcations between the groups of data.

MEMO

Plot Series On? What's that? Excel allows you to plot some series on the primary axis and some on the secondary. The primary axis for a bar chart is the bottom axis; secondary is the top axis. Changing series plotting from one to the other will make the chart better if there is a wide range of values for some sets of data compared to others. Be aware that if you have adjusted the gap or overlap for the series, it will return to the defaults when you change its axis. There is another gotcha involved with secondary axes. When you move data to the second axis, the bars show on top of the primary axis bars. Excel automatically centers the content of the secondary axis over the cluster of bars for the primary axis. This will change how the gaps for the bars work.

The default settings for gaps and overlaps actually make a lot of sense. Use them most of the time for the best possible charts. Only adjust them if the change makes the chart more readable or more understandable.

Legends (Not Screen Ones, the Ones on Your Charts)

The legend for your chart is the roadmap connecting the colors/fills for each bar to the series name associated with that bar. Changing how a bar looks changes the legend as well.

By default, legends are visible to the far right of the bar chart. You can change the location of the legend either by picking a different chart layout or by formatting the legend itself. As a starting point, let's look at where the layouts put the legend:

- Layout 1 places the legend to the right of the chart as a vertical list.

- Layout 2 places the legend between the title and the chart as a horizontal list.

- Layouts 3 and 4 place the legend below the chart as a horizontal list.

- Layouts 5 and 6 turn off the legend.

If you have the labels for the bars turned on, you probably don't need a legend. Be careful with this, though—labels on the bars of a busy chart can cause more confusion than they solve.

Right-clicking the legend and selecting Format allows you to use the Format Legend dialog to change where your legend resides and how it looks. Four of the option pages here should look familiar: Fill, Border Color, Border Styles, and Shadow all work the same as on any other chart element. Legend Options allows you to customize where the legend sits, as shown in Figure 2-9.

Once you have decided which of the five positions you like, you have one more decision to make. You need to decide whether the legend should be able to overlap the data. While overlapping the legend and the data can work, in general, it detracts from the clarity of your chart.

You can adjust the spacing of the legend items by dragging the handles on the legend. This will resize the legend box. Excel will then set up a best-fit layout for the legend items.

If you want to adjust the text formatting for your legend, select the legend and use the text-formatting options on the Home tab. Since the default font size for the legend is only 10 point, you are likely to find yourself making this change frequently.

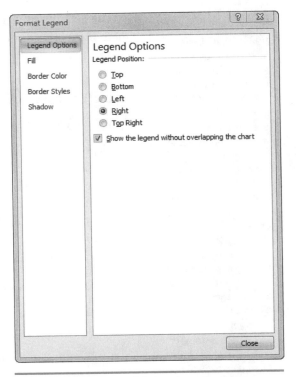

Figure 2-9   Format Legend dialog – legend options

MEMO

What if I want my legend somewhere besides at the edge? If you uncheck the box restricting the legend from overlapping the data, you can drag the legend to any open space on your chart. If you have a large block of white space in your chart, moving and manually adjusting the size of the legend can reduce the size of your chart area.

Changing the Data Range

One of the nicest charting features in Excel 2007 allows you to quickly and easily change which data shows in your chart. Using the Chart Tools | Design | Select Data button, you can add, remove, or change series and categories of data, as shown in Figure 2-10.

The left side of the dialog allows you to change which series are in your chart. The names of the series are taken directly from the data.

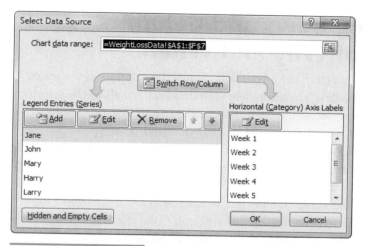

Figure 2-10 Select Data Source

Removing a series is a simple matter of selecting the series name in the left panel and clicking the Remove button. Adding and editing the data for the chart is slightly more complicated. Click the name of one of the series of data, and click the Add button. A small dialog will pop up that contains the formula for the series name, value, its values, and four buttons.

OK and Cancel are pretty straightforward. OK applies the changes you have made, while Cancel discards them. The grid buttons are where the power sits. If you click the grid button for the name, you can change the cell that has the name of this series in it. You can even edit the value and replace the formula with your own text. Clicking the grid button for the series itself allows you to either type a new series range or drag in your data to select different data.

To add a new set of data to your chart, click the Add button. Set the label for the series by activating the data sheet and clicking the cell with the series name. Set the range for the new series by activating the data sheet and selecting the data range you want to use. When you have set both the name and the range for the new series, click OK twice, and your new data range will appear in the chart.

To change the order of the data in your chart, select the series name to move, and use the up and down arrows to the right of the Remove button. As you change the order, you will see the change in your chart. If you don't like the changes, click the Cancel button to discard them.

At the lower-left area of the dialog, there is a button marked Hidden and Empty Cells. Clicking this button brings up a dialog that lets you choose how to show your empty data cells (as gaps or zeros for bar and column charts), as well as whether you want to show the data in hidden rows and columns.

THE EASY WAY

Accidentally include data in your chart that you don't want? Use this dialog to remove that entire series or those elements of the series from the chart.

33

Switching Rows and Columns – Details of Why and When

When Excel creates a chart from your data, it puts the columns as the series and the rows as the data. Unfortunately, your data may not always be set up that way. You already know how to fix it—click the Swap Rows/Columns button. But how do you decide which way to build your chart?

When you create your data, you naturally create it in the easiest way to add data. Usually, this also shows the relationship you think is most important. In the weight loss data case, you have a set number of people participating, but the number of weeks could change. It makes sense to make the people the columns and the weeks the rows. When you look at the chart, you want to see how each person did, not how much was lost each week. This is a case where the data would need to be swapped.

On the other hand, if the weight loss had been tracked over a year, with monthly weigh-ins, it would be easier to set up the columns as the months and the people as the rows. Since there are 12 months in a year, this setup allows the column headings to be preset and the people to expand if needed. In that case, the data would be set up correctly for the chart and you wouldn't need to swap it.

Swapping is also useful if you don't know which way you want to chart the data. Switching rows and columns can sometimes show things you don't expect. In this case, looking at the weight loss charts by date instead of person would allow you to see if there were any weeks during which everyone lost weight or everyone gained weight.

Saving Your Chart as a Template

Now that you have the perfect setup for your bar chart, wouldn't it be nice to be able to reuse it quickly and easily? You can! Click Chart Tools | Design | Save As Template. A Save dialog will appear with the Excel chart template folder open. Give the template a unique and descriptive name, and click Save. A new .crtx file will be created.

To use the new chart template, create a chart and use the Chart Tools | Design | Change Chart Type button to bring up the list of available templates. Once you save your first chart template, a new entry will appear at the top of your chart type list: Templates. This folder will show all of the chart templates you have created using Excel 2007.

Creating and Formatting a Basic Line Chart

Line charts help show trends in your data. They show the progression from one data point to the next. Where bar and column charts compare sets of information, line charts help show what changes were gone through to get to where you are today. Line charts tend to have more data points on them than bar and column charts, because these charts show the flow of information instead of a series of individual states.

One use for a line chart is to compare sales by individuals over time. The opening illustration shows the number of houses sold by a few realtors over a period of 12 months. Over this time, each realtor had their ups and downs. The high sales months and the low sales months can be seen, as they could with the bar and column charts. The line chart also shows that while everyone had slow sales months, most of the slow months were followed by high sales months.

The line chart can show relationships between multiple series of data. In this case, you can see that Lon was always the top seller and Terrance was always the low seller.

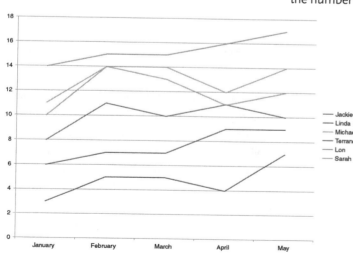

While there might be specific reasons for this, it leads you down the road to knowing who needs help and who doesn't. By looking at the data in a line chart, the difference between these two sellers jumps out at the viewer.

Line charts also help predict where the data will go next by adding trend lines to the data. Trend lines show the general progression of your data from one period to the next. Trend lines can be misleading, however—you will read more about that in a bit.

Creating the Chart from Data

The first step in creating any chart is to determine what data you are going to chart. Figure 3-1 shows the data used to create the charts in this chapter. This data can be found in the file Chapter3HousesSold.xlsx.

	A	B	C	D	E	F	G	H	I	J	K	L	M
1	Name	January	February	March	April	May	June	July	August	September	October	November	December
2	Jackie	8	11	10	11	10	9	12	11	9	10	11	11
3	Linda	6	7	7	9	9	8	10	7	9	7	10	9
4	Michael	11	14	14	12	14	12	13	12	13	15	14	12
5	Terrance	3	5	5	4	7	6	5	5	6	6	5	5
6	Lon	14	15	15	16	17	17	17	15	16	17	18	18
7	Sarah	10	14	13	11	12	12	11	13	14	13	11	13
8													
9													

Figure 3-1   Data table – houses sold by realtors over a year

In this format, it is hard to do any evaluations on how the various realtors did over the year. It is hard to compare the results between months, let alone between realtors. However, by converting this data to a line chart, some comparisons jump out at the viewer. In this case, the entire set of data can be charted and then the rows and columns swapped. When this is done, it immediately becomes obvious that every time a realtor has an off month, they follow it with a great sales month.

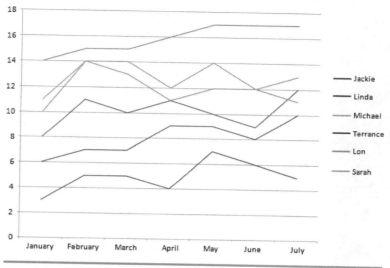

Figure 3-2 Line chart of houses sold

To create the line chart shown in Figure 3-2, select the sales data for all six realtors for the first six months of the year. Click Insert | Line, and select the first chart in the gallery. Use Chart Tools | Design | Move Chart to move the chart to its own sheet. Then, use Chart Tools | Design | Switch Row/Column to see the data by realtor instead of by month.

This is a basic line chart. There are a few formatting things you can do to make the chart look nicer. One of these changes is to make the markers for the data points more visible. That will be covered later in the chapter.

Changing a Bar or Column Chart to a Line Chart

Bar and column charts are great for comparing certain kinds of data. However, when too much data is plotted, the extra bars quickly clutter up the chart. A column chart of the sales for three of the realtors shows how the realtors did each month, but it is hard to tell how their sales compared over time.

THE LANGUAGE OF CHARTING

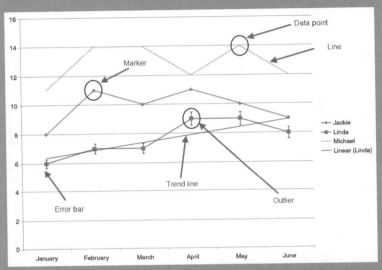

Charts have a language all their own. They use terms that are common in the rest of the world, but they have their own specific meanings in the Excel charting world.

- **Point or data point** The spot on the chart that represents an individual data point in a series.

- **Line** Connection between points on a line chart. May be straight or curved, depending on the chart.

- **Marker** A picture or shape that shows the data point.

- **Trend** A prediction of future results based on the current information.

- **Trend line** Line in a line chart that plots the trend for a specific series of data.

- **Outlier** A point that sits outside of the smooth curve of the rest of the data.

- **Error bars** Small lines ranging up and down from an individual data point, showing the potential error for the current data point.

You can't see the flow or learn at a glance any trends from the data when it is shown in a column chart as in Figure 3-3.

On the other hand, when this same data is charted as a line chart, the data points are clearer. As shown in Figure 3-4, the lines allow visualization of the peaks and valleys for each realtor, as well as whether each is getting better or worse over time.

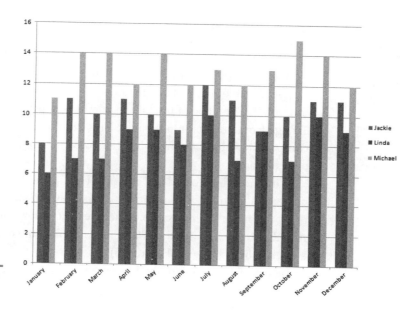

Figure 3-3   Column chart for three realtors

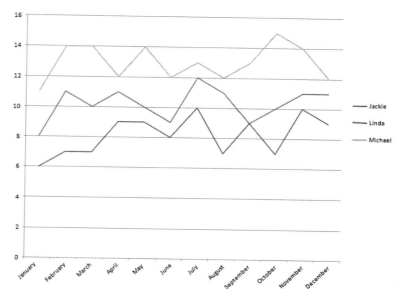

Figure 3-4   Line chart for three realtors

THE EASY WAY

Right-click any chart, and you can change it to any other chart type or subtype. Some of the charts may not make much sense, but you can always do the change.

Types of Line Charts

When you think "line chart," you probably think of a chart with lines going from point to point in the series. The lines for the different series may intersect each other, or a single point may have more than one line going through it. The slope of the line segments is dependent on the amount of change from one point to the next. This kind of line chart is typically used to compare how the data for each series compares to the data for the other series on the chart.

With the ability to add and remove series from the chart easily, basic line charts can tell quite a bit about the data. They can show progression over time or place. In the realtor example, the lines show how each realtor did each month. But there is another way you can look at the data in a line chart: using a stacked line chart (see Figure 3-5).

In a stacked line chart, the lines are shown as a sum of a whole. Each series is shown as a layer within the whole. This allows you to show how

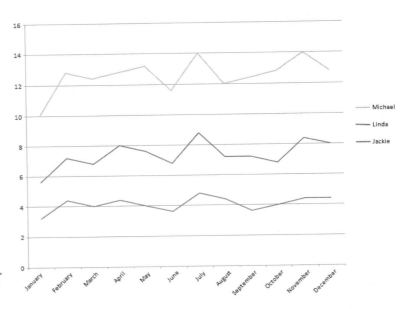

Figure 3-5 Stacked line chart for three realtors

things changed for each series over the period of the chart, as well as how things progressed in the big picture. They are commonly used for comparisons between total values across all series.

When the realtor data is shown as a stacked chart, as in Figure 3-5, not only can the sales of each individual be seen, but the total sales for the office is seen, too. While the individual lines show that dips were followed by highs for the realtors, the stacked chart shows that everyone had an off month in June and August. While you can see this in the regular chart, the stacked chart shows it much more clearly.

There is a third kind of line chart, called a 100% Stacked chart. In this type of chart, the sales are converted to percentages of the whole. You might look at this as a series of pie charts unrolled. Each data point is a segment of one pie chart, with the series showing how each realtor's sales compared to the whole (see Figure 3-6). Here, the peaks and valleys are evened out a bit, since they have been converted from actual numbers to parts of the whole.

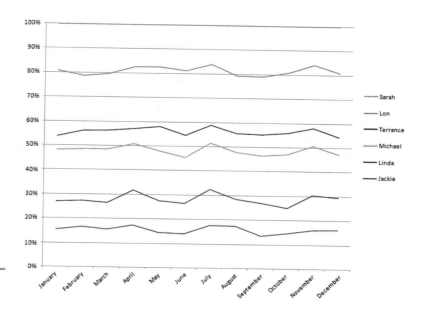

Figure 3-6   100% Stacked line chart

44

MEMO

You can only create one kind of 3-D line chart: a plain, unmarked chart. While this may seem like a creative idea, it usually isn't. A 3-D line chart can quickly become confusing and misleading. Build one for yourself and see.

THE EASY WAY

If you want to have markers for some lines but not for all, stay with the regular line chart types. Select the series that you want to have markers, and turn them on individually. This isn't easier if you want all the lines to have markers, but it is easier if only some lines will have markers.

One of the things the 100% Stacked chart shows is that Lon's sales are always a higher percentage of the whole than anyone else's. The gap representing his sales is always larger than any other gap in the chart. From this we learn that even in an off month, Lon's sales are still a significant percentage of the office's total.

By the way, if you think you have a need for a stacked line chart, you probably don't. In general, data that is shown as a stacked line chart is really data that should be shown as an area chart. You can learn more about area charts by reading Chapter 5.

Markers and What They Mean

On a default line chart, the data points are not called out in any particular way. If there is an abrupt change in the direction of the data from one point to the next, there will be a sharp bend in the line; other than that, the only indication of the actual data point is the intersection between the two axes.

In some cases, this is fine. If you are looking for a trend in the data, you probably don't want to call attention to the exact data points. On the other hand, if what you are trying to show is the relationship between the values, you will want to turn on the markers for your data points.

Markers are indicators of the exact value of the data point. In our realtor data, they are the intersection between the month of the sales and the number of houses sold (see Figure 3-7). If you wanted to see the data points more clearly, you would turn on the markers by changing the chart type to one of the three types with markers.

By default, each line gets a unique shape for its marker. To change the shapes for the markers, select the series and bring up the Format dialog. Select the Marker Options section, as shown in Figure 3-8.

This dialog lets you change from the automatic bullets to no bullets to a custom bullet of your choice. Most of the custom bullets are basic shapes. Whether you want to customize the markers for one line or all lines, you will need to do the customization one line at a time. When you select a shape

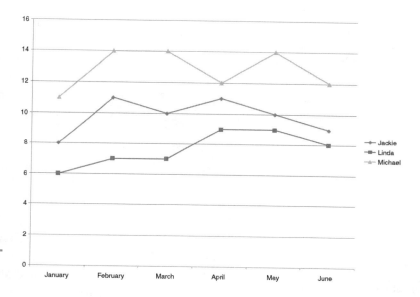

Figure 3-7 Line chart
with markers

specifically for your marker, you can also adjust the size of the marker.
You can't adjust the size of the automatic markers.

Once you have chosen the shape and size for your marker, use the options
under Marker Fill to make them just what you desire, as shown in Figure 3-9.

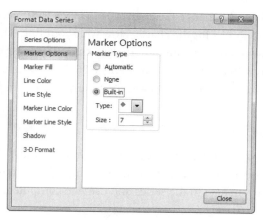

The options for your
marker fills are the same as
for any other fill in Office
2007. You can set them to a
solid color, a gradient, or
a picture fill. If you choose a
picture fill from here, the
picture will be shrunk to fit
the size of the marker. If you
have overlapping lines, you
can also use the options here
to set the transparency for the

Figure 3-8 Format Data
Series dialog with Marker
Options area showing

46

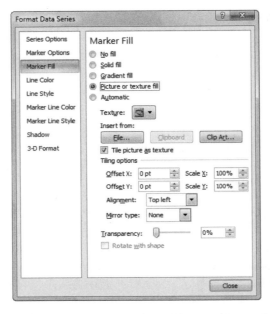

Figure 3-9 Format Data Series dialog with Marker Fill options for picture or texture fills showing

MEMO

At the bottom of the built-in marker types, there is an option to change your marker to a picture placeholder. I do not recommend doing this. This option replaces each marker with a picture placeholder. When you click the picture placeholder and select a new picture for the marker, you end up with full-size copies of the picture for your marker. You are unable to adjust the marker size, so the markers quickly take over your chart.

markers so that you can see any underlying markers. A great use of picture marker fills is to show who or what the data represents. If each line's marker was a picture of the realtor represented by the line, you could eliminate the legend from the chart.

If you are using a custom fill for your marker, make sure that the marker is big enough to show. You may need to even use the Marker Line Color and Marker Line Style options to adjust the lines to allow the marker fill to show.

When you set up your markers, remember that they do add extra elements to your line chart. If you have many data points on many lines, don't use complicated markers for each line. You will end up with a cluttered chart that is hard to read.

When you change the chart type to Lines with Markers, the styles also adjust the line widths for the charts. How wide your lines should be depends, in part, on how many lines you have in your chart. If you have only a few lines, you can go with a heavier line, as in Style 26. But if you have more than a couple of lines, you are not going to want to go any wider than what is shown in Style 18.

Adding and Using Trend Lines

Once you have a general idea of what your data says about the current situation, trend lines are used to show what might happen in the future. Trend lines take the current data in the series and use it to compute the future data values.

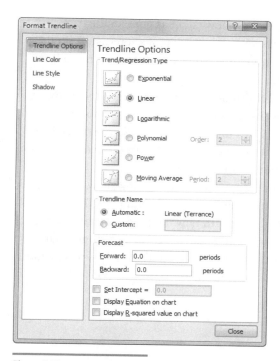

Figure 3-10   Format Trendline dialog

Once you have a line chart created, trend lines are added via Chart Tools | Layout | Trendline (see Figure 3-10). If you have a line or series selected when you select a trend line from the list, that trend line will be applied to the selected line. You can access four types of trend lines directly from the ribbon:

- **Linear trend**   A straight line that plots the beginning point and the end point, and predicts the future trend based on those two points.

- **Exponential trend**   A curving trend line, where the points between the first and last points are taken into consideration. Several versions are available in Excel. Generally, an exponential trend is more accurate than a linear trend.

- **Linear forecast**   Straight line trending from the first point to the last point and on into the future two more months (data points).

- **Moving average**   Determines the trend based on the last two data points. Starts two data points in from the beginning of the line. This is a good way to tell if your data is following a linear predictive model. The closer the line follows your data, the better predictor the trend line will be.

In addition to the trend lines you can add from the ribbon, you can add more types of trend lines from the Format Trendline dialog. The last option on the trendline list, More Trendline Options, activates the dialog.

The Format Trendline dialog gives you more flexibility in creating trend lines. Beyond the four basic lines available from the ribbon, you can also create polynomial trend lines and power trend lines. Polynomial trend lines take the points and use a polynomic formula to determine the next value for the trend line. Power trend lines are approximations of the trend across the entire series.

THE EASY WAY

If you don't have a line or series selected when you go to add a trend line, a dialog will appear that lists the series in the chart. You may find this the easier way to add your trend lines.

MEMO

A polynomial trend line with an order of 2 is close to the same as a linear trend line. The larger the number for the polynomial, the closer the fit will be to your actual data. The maximum value for the order is 6. However, if you extend a polynomial trend line into the future, it will quickly become a bad predictor of reality.

At their most basic, trend lines show how data has gone in the past. The power of the trend line comes with the addition of a forecast. With the exception of the moving average trend line, you can extend your trend lines into both the past and the future.

One of the best ways to learn how trend lines work as predictors is to see them on a chart. Figure 3-11 has the sales data for the first six months of the year for each realtor. Each realtor has a different type of trend line attached. For those trend lines that can be used as predictors, the trend lines have been set to show the sales for three months in the future.

The last two check boxes on the Format Trendline dialog allow you to show both the equation and the R-squared values for your trend lines. These two options are useful if you will need to explain how the predictive curves were created. Be aware, though, that adding too many of these to a single chart can make the chart unreadable. You may want to put these items in separate documentation rather than on the chart itself.

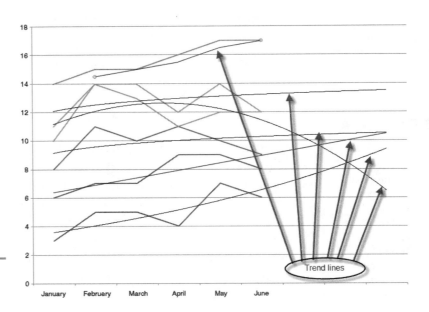

Figure 3-11   Realtor sales data with future prediction trend lines

MEMO

On the Format tab, you will find a button labeled Selection Pane. One would hope that this pane would allow you to select the parts of your chart. It does not. It allows you to select the chart and any additional objects you have placed on the chart or data page.

To remove a trend line that you have added, select the line and select None from the trend line gallery. You can't remove a trend line from the Format Trendline dialog, nor can you change it to have a line color of none.

Formatting Chart Parts

Just as with any other chart, you can select and format any piece of a line chart by either clicking the item or using the Current Selection list. If you don't like the way you have changed an item, you can reset it by clicking Chart Tools | Layout | Reset to Match Style or Chart Tools | Format | Reset to Match Style.

In addition, you can change how the lines look on your chart by selecting them and choosing a line style from the Chart Tools | Format | Shape Styles gallery.

What if your chart was showing the income for each realtor instead of the number of houses sold? Because the numbers would be much higher, it would be nice to change the axis to show the income in millions of dollars instead of just dollars (see Figure 3-12).

This chart is nice, but because the sales figures are so high, the numbers become hard to read at a glance. It would be easier to understand the values in this chart if they were shown as millions of dollars instead of just dollars.

To change the axis, select the Vertical (Value) Axis from the current selection list. Click the Format button to bring up the Format Axis dialog. The first page of options, the Axis Options, allows you to change how the values on this axis are shown, as shown in Figure 3-13.

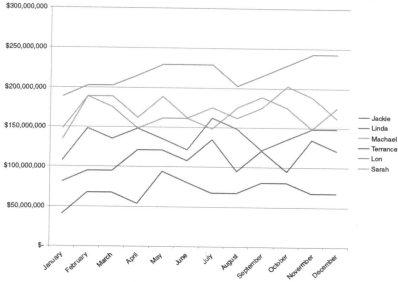

Figure 3-12   Unadjusted axis

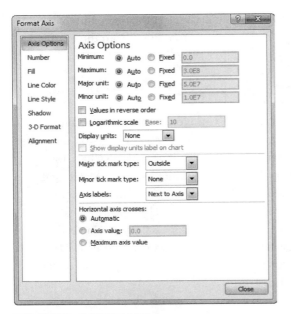

About halfway down the dialog, there is a drop-down list for Display Units. Change the value from None to Millions. Instantly, the graph changes to a scope the viewer's brain can more easily comprehend (see Figure 3-14). Changing the display units also allows you to turn on or off the display units. In most cases, it is a good idea to keep the display units visible to increase the clarity of your chart.

Primary and Secondary Axes

If the data on your line chart is not all within the same range of data, charting it all on one axis can create an unusable chart. Imagine that you wanted to compare

Figure 3-13   Format Axis
dialog, Axis options

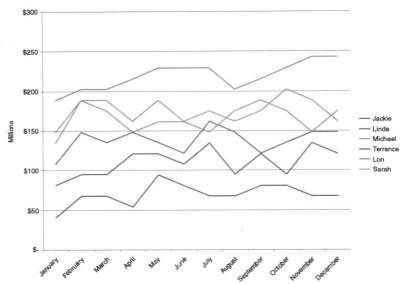

Figure 3-14   Adjusted axis
showing data in millions
instead of dollars

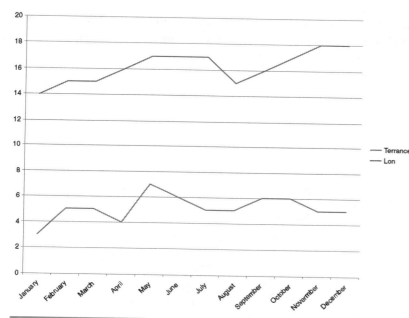

Figure 3-15   Lon and
Terrance on a single axis

how Lon and Terrance did over the year. You know that Lon sold many more houses each month than Terrance, but you are curious as to how closely the plot of the data would compare. If you plot both sets of data on the same axis, you get a chart with a wide space between the two sets of data, as shown in Figure 3-15.

This is nice, but it would be even better if the lines were closer together so that you could spot the matches and the disjointed information. To do this, you would move one of the lines to a second axis.

Select Lon's line and activate the Format dialog. On the first set of options, change from plotting the data on the primary axis to the secondary axis. When you do this, the two lines move closer together. Now, the ranges of data are overlaid so that you can compare the work of both realtors. The resulting chart points out something interesting: Not only did Lon sell more houses, he was more consistent in his sales and progressively sold more as the year went on. Terrance, on the other hand, was all over the map in his sales. The slope of his line was always much steeper than Lon's, showing that his performance changed more drastically as time went on.

Combine this idea with the amount of income from houses, and you have a powerful chart. Put Lon back on the primary axis. Add the data to the chart showing the sales income for the two realtors. Place the income

THE EASY WAY

Once there are two axes set up for your data, you can change the display units to one of the most common values by using Chart Tools | Layout | Axes | Secondary Vertical Axis, and selecting the display units you want from the list.

on the secondary axis. Change the display units to millions. Notice that now the chart shows twice as much data, without adding much more confusion (see Figure 3-16).

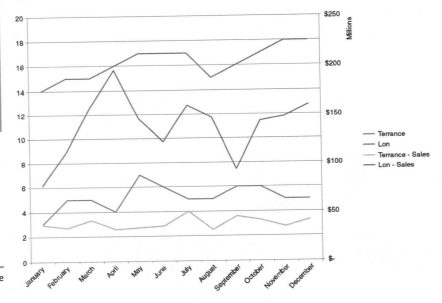

Figure 3-16   Lon and Terrance sales and income chart

Creating and Formatting a Basic Pie Chart

The ubiquitous pie chart. You find them everywhere, from charity reports showing how much of the income actually went to the charity, to what fruit pies people like the most. Good ones show at a glance exactly what the chart creator wants seen. Bad ones make your data less understandable than just looking at the raw data.

At its most basic, a pie chart is a circle with each piece showing a different part of the whole. The chart itself shows the whole of the data, while each piece shows the percentage of the total represented by the label. The best of the pies show at a glance the relationships between the various pieces and the whole.

Pie charts are some of the first charts many users make. While not the default chart (that's the column chart), it is the chart most easily created from data. Pie charts only work with one row of data, so there is no worry about what goes where. And since they are based on a food item everyone knows of, they are easily understood.

Votes

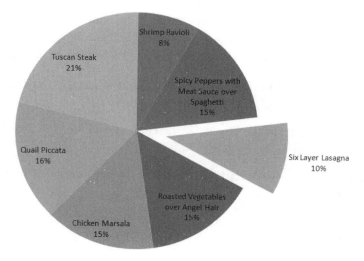

Pie charts should only be used for those situations where there is one line of data and where each piece of data represents a part of the whole. If the data can be looked at as a percentage of something, then it is made for a pie chart. If it is comparing results across time, then it probably isn't. For example, looking at raw data from a survey as a line or bar chart will help you see where trends are. Looking at that data in a pie chart will help you see which items were most important.

Creating the Chart from Data

When creating a pie chart, you are asking Excel to look at the selected cells and provide a picture of how each value relates to the sum of all the values. Unlike other charts, you are only going to be working with one row of data when creating your pie charts. The data for a sample pie chart is shown in Figure 4-1.

This data shows the results of a promotion to add a new item to Jackie's Restaurant. Looking at this data, you can tell some of the story already. You can see which were the highest and lowest vote-getters. What a pie chart is going to be bringing to the table is an easy way to compare the results for each dish.

Potential Items	Votes
Shrimp Ravioli	10
Spicy Peppers with Meat Sauce over Spaghetti	18
Six Layer Lasagna	12
Roasted Vegetables over Angel Hair	18
Chicken Marsala	18
Quail Piccata	20
Tuscan Steak	26

Figure 4-1 An Excel 2007 table

1. Open the Excel 2007 file Chap4FavoriteMenuItems.xlsx. The first page of data contains the table shown in Figure 4-1.

2. Select any cell that contains data, and click Insert | Pie | Pie. The new chart will appear on the sheet.

3. Click Design | Move Chart, and move the chart to a new page in the data (see Figure 4-2).

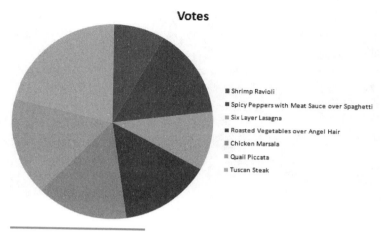

Votes

- Shrimp Ravioli
- Spicy Peppers with Meat Sauce over Spaghetti
- Six Layer Lasagna
- Roasted Vegetables over Angel Hair
- Chicken Marsala
- Quail Piccata
- Tuscan Steak

Figure 4-2   The basic pie chart

Each piece of the pie chart represents one recipe. To the right of the pie is a legend that shows the correlation between the colors and the recipes. For a simple chart like this one, the legend is making the reader work hard to learn what the chart is saying. For a chart like this, it is often better to put the labels and the values on the actual pieces themselves. The quickest way to make this change is to apply a different layout to the chart.

THE LANGUAGE OF CHARTING

Charts have a language all their own. They use terms that are common in the rest of the world, but they have their own specific meanings in the Excel charting world.

- **Pie**   Circular chart that shows the data points as percentages of a whole.

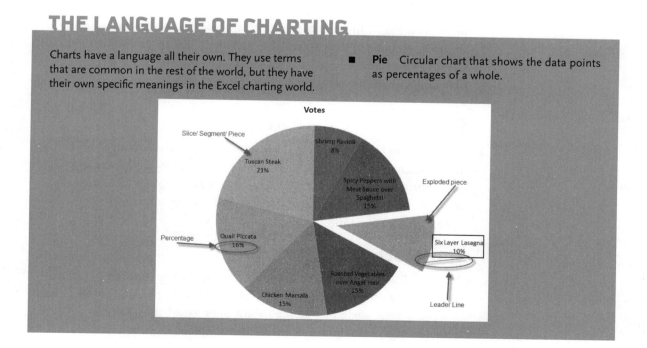

THE LANGUAGE OF CHARTING (CONT.)

- **Slice or segment** The pie piece that represents an individual data point's percentage of the total.

- **Exploded pie** A pie chart where the pieces are pulled away from the center so that there is a gap around some or all of the pieces.

- **Rotation** The number of degrees the pie has been rotated off center. By default, the first data element has a rotation of zero degrees and shows as the top or 12:00 slice.

By changing the rotation, other slices can become the 12:00 slice.

- **Leader lines** Lines used to connect labels off the chart with the pie slice on the chart.

- **Percentage** Percentage of the whole represented by this particular slice. By default, percentages are rounded to whole numbers. This can be changed via the Format Series dialog.

Applying pie chart layout Layout1 to this chart will move the data labels onto each pie piece. In addition, it will add the percentage of the whole each slice represents to the data label. That gets the chart a step closer to being understandable. Unfortunately, the font size for the labels is quite small. To fix that, select one of the labels. Click the Home | Font Size drop-down list, and change the font size to 14. This will change the font to the largest size that easily fits within each of the slices.

Pie Chart Limitations

There are two big limitations to how you create pie charts, both of which are related to having too much data for the chart. If you have too many data points, the pie chart will be many tiny slices, none of which are really comprehendible. The second problem is that you can only chart one row or column of data at a time.

Too Much Data

We have all seen them. The pie charts that have 20 segments (or more) and all of them are so small that you can't tell what is going on. While these charts do a really great job of pretending to be a color wheel, they don't do a good job of sharing useful information. As an example, if the menu voting had

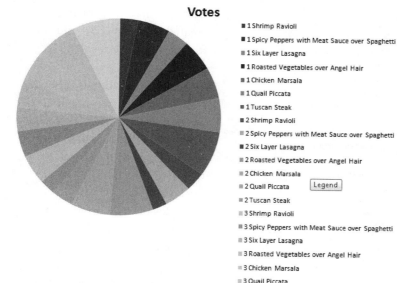

Votes

- 1 Shrimp Ravioli
- 1 Spicy Peppers with Meat Sauce over Spaghetti
- 1 Six Layer Lasagna
- 1 Roasted Vegetables over Angel Hair
- 1 Chicken Marsala
- 1 Quail Piccata
- 1 Tuscan Steak
- 2 Shrimp Ravioli
- 2 Spicy Peppers with Meat Sauce over Spaghetti
- 2 Six Layer Lasagna
- 2 Roasted Vegetables over Angel Hair
- 2 Chicken Marsala
- 2 Quail Piccata   Legend
- 2 Tuscan Steak
- 3 Shrimp Ravioli
- 3 Spicy Peppers with Meat Sauce over Spaghetti
- 3 Six Layer Lasagna
- 3 Roasted Vegetables over Angel Hair
- 3 Chicken Marsala
- 3 Quail Piccata
- 3 Tuscan Steak

Figure 4-3   The overloaded pie chart

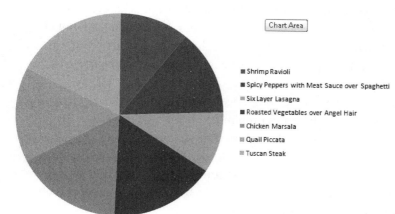

Chart Area

- Shrimp Ravioli
- Spicy Peppers with Meat Sauce over Spaghetti
- Six Layer Lasagna
- Roasted Vegetables over Angel Hair
- Chicken Marsala
- Quail Piccata
- Tuscan Steak

Figure 4-4   The totaled chart

gone on for three weeks, it might be tempting to create a pie chart showing how the votes went each week. The results? See Figure 4-3.

Here, you can see that the first and second rows were taken as labels for the data and the third row is taken as the data. Without any kind of numeric labeling, all the pieces start to blend together when you look at the chart. There is a temptation to change the style to one with percentages or values showing. Don't do it. Or, better yet, do it once and then once you see the results, never do it again.

What's a charter to do? Sometimes, there is just going to be too much data for one chart. Instead of breaking the votes down by week, group your data and chart the grouped data. Some data detail is lost, but since the chart will be clearer, much understanding will be gained. Sometimes, what you need to do is clean up and combine data pieces so that the pie chart you build is clearer. To do this, create a series of formulas that adds up the votes each recipe got and places the result in a new cell.

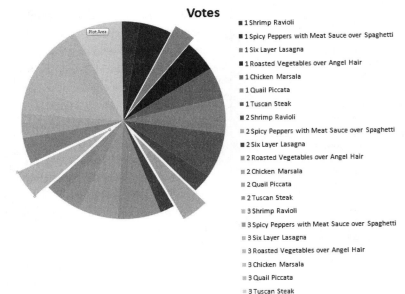

Votes

- 1 Shrimp Ravioli
- 1 Spicy Peppers with Meat Sauce over Spaghetti
- 1 Six Layer Lasagna
- 1 Roasted Vegetables over Angel Hair
- 1 Chicken Marsala
- 1 Quail Piccata
- 1 Tuscan Steak
- 2 Shrimp Ravioli
- 2 Spicy Peppers with Meat Sauce over Spaghetti
- 2 Six Layer Lasagna
- 2 Roasted Vegetables over Angel Hair
- 2 Chicken Marsala
- 2 Quail Piccata
- 2 Tuscan Steak
- 3 Shrimp Ravioli
- 3 Spicy Peppers with Meat Sauce over Spaghetti
- 3 Six Layer Lasagna
- 3 Roasted Vegetables over Angel Hair
- 3 Chicken Marsala
- 3 Quail Piccata
- 3 Tuscan Steak

Figure 4-5   Lasagna slices expanded

Once you have the formulas created, you can chart and format that. The result? See Figure 4-4.

A second solution is to set off some of the segments so that they are exploded outward. Exploded pieces are those that have been pulled out from the center so that they stand out from the rest of the data.

Explosion is done either by dragging the pieces of the chart out from the center of the pie or by selecting the pieces and using the Format | Series Options section.

To move the pieces out by hand, select the piece and drag it out from the center. The other pieces will move away from the piece, and it will slide out. A space will be left around the slice. This works fine when exploding one slice, but is harder to get right when more than one slice needs to be moved out. Because the amount of movement depends not just on the slide of the mouse, but also on the size of the slice, it is harder to get the spacing consistent across all the moved slices (see Figure 4-5).

If slices that are next to each other need to be exploded, the problems with dragging them by hand becomes even more obvious. Dragging out the Spicy Peppers slice from week one shows how difficult it is to line slices up by eye (see Figure 4-6). Try it.

Notice that the slice doesn't look as cleanly moved as the slices near it. Even though only the one slice was moved, the two near it also seem to be more out of balance than when it was still centered.

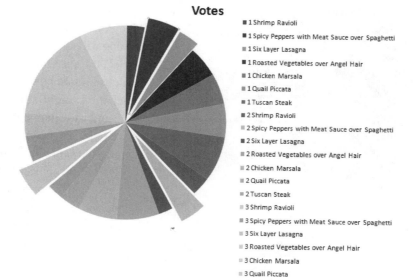

Figure 4-6   Lasagna slices plus one Spicy Peppers slice expanded

THE EASY WAY

Use the Format dialog. Adjusting all slices out from the center becomes a single change when using the Format dialog. Adjusting multiple slices is still tricky, but it is easier to undo what was done and get things right. Start by selecting the Spicy Peppers slice from week one. Right-click and select Format Data Point. The options on this dialog (shown in Figure 4-7) will allow you to adjust the single slice to where you need it to be.

Figure 4-7   The Format Data Point dialog with the Series Options area showing

Votes

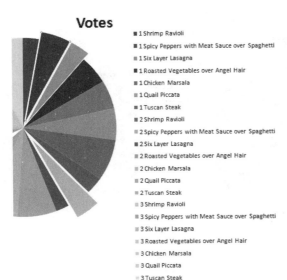

- 1 Shrimp Ravioli
- 1 Spicy Peppers with Meat Sauce over Spaghetti
- 1 Six Layer Lasagna
- 1 Roasted Vegetables over Angel Hair
- 1 Chicken Marsala
- 1 Quail Piccata
- 1 Tuscan Steak
- 2 Shrimp Ravioli
- 2 Spicy Peppers with Meat Sauce over Spaghetti
- 2 Six Layer Lasagna
- 2 Roasted Vegetables over Angel Hair
- 2 Chicken Marsala
- 2 Quail Piccata
- 2 Tuscan Steak
- 3 Shrimp Ravioli
- 3 Spicy Peppers with Meat Sauce over Spaghetti
- 3 Six Layer Lasagna
- 3 Roasted Vegetables over Angel Hair
- 3 Chicken Marsala
- 3 Quail Piccata
- 3 Tuscan Steak

Figure 4-8 Pie chart with two consecutive pieces exploded

MEMO

If only one piece moves out, even though you had all the slices selected, you need to reset the formatting on the graph. Select the series, and then use Chart Tools | Format | Reset to Match Style to reset the slices. After that, dragging one slice out will drag all the slices out.

To adjust how far out the piece is exploded, use the Point Explosion slider. As pieces are selected, the dialog will change to show the values for that piece. Select the slice for Spicy Peppers for week one. The results should be similar to the dialog shown. If you click the Lasagna slice for week one, you will see its rate and can change it. Set the rate for the Lasagna slice to be 15 percent by either moving the slider or typing the value in the box.

Even if two pieces have the same explosion value, the pieces will not have the same layout. Because the explosion percentage depends on both the size of the selected piece and the sizes of the pieces next to it, having the same value for two pieces does not move them out the same amount. Select the Spicy Peppers piece again, and change it to the same number as the Lasagna piece and the chart will change to what is shown in Figure 4-8.

Notice that the pieces don't quite look right? Exploding consecutive pieces isn't going to get you a better chart. In this case, it is going to get you a chart where the eye catches on the pieces that are exploded, but also where the eye notices that the explosions are not correct.

Instead, if there has to be a large number of slices, consider exploding all pieces. To do this, select the series instead of the individual data points. Drag any piece out, and the others will move the right amount as well (see Figure 4-9).

The other solution is to create a bar of pie or pie of pie chart. These will be covered at the end of this chapter. These are special pie charts that pull the values of a group of slices together as a single slice and then add a second chart with the breakdown of the individual data pieces.

Multiple Rows

The order of the information you want to chart affects how the final chart looks. If you have multiple rows of data, the pie chart you get will not be what you

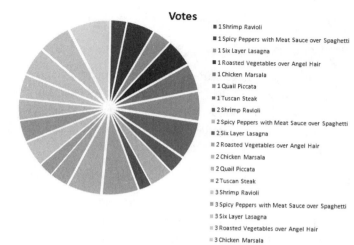

Votes

- 1 Shrimp Ravioli
- 1 Spicy Peppers with Meat Sauce over Spaghetti
- 1 Six Layer Lasagna
- 1 Roasted Vegetables over Angel Hair
- 1 Chicken Marsala
- 1 Quail Piccata
- 1 Tuscan Steak
- 2 Shrimp Ravioli
- 2 Spicy Peppers with Meat Sauce over Spaghetti
- 2 Six Layer Lasagna
- 2 Roasted Vegetables over Angel Hair
- 2 Chicken Marsala
- 2 Quail Piccata
- 2 Tuscan Steak
- 3 Shrimp Ravioli
- 3 Spicy Peppers with Meat Sauce over Spaghetti
- 3 Six Layer Lasagna
- 3 Roasted Vegetables over Angel Hair
- 3 Chicken Marsala
- 3 Quail Piccata
- 3 Tuscan Steak

Figure 4-9   All pieces exploded

are expecting. Pie charts can only handle one row of data. If more than one row is selected, Excel 2007 will create a slice for each data element in the first row and ignore the data in the second row.

Figure 4-10 shows what happens when you try to chart two rows of data in pie chart. It almost looks like it might have done what was desired, doesn't it? If the data in the second row is changed, nothing changes in the chart. This proves that only the first row of data is being charted.

What can be done? One solution is to re-order the data so that one set of the data becomes the label instead of the data. Another solution is to use a Pivot Chart. Pivot Charts will be covered in Chapter 12.

61

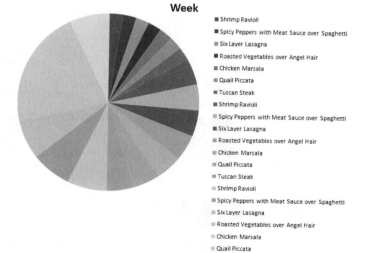

Week

- Shrimp Ravioli
- Spicy Peppers with Meat Sauce over Spaghetti
- Six Layer Lasagna
- Roasted Vegetables over Angel Hair
- Chicken Marsala
- Quail Piccata
- Tuscan Steak
- Shrimp Ravioli
- Spicy Peppers with Meat Sauce over Spaghetti
- Six Layer Lasagna
- Roasted Vegetables over Angel Hair
- Chicken Marsala
- Quail Piccata
- Tuscan Steak
- Shrimp Ravioli
- Spicy Peppers with Meat Sauce over Spaghetti
- Six Layer Lasagna
- Roasted Vegetables over Angel Hair
- Chicken Marsala
- Quail Piccata
- Tuscan Steak

Figure 4-10   Attempt to chart two rows of data

MEMO

Unlike most of the other chart types, there is not a predefined layout that shows the data table. This is because with a single line of data, there is no need to show the data table. If the values are to be shown, they are shown as part of the label for the pieces.

Formatting Your Chart with the Built-in Styles and Layouts

Chart styles and layouts help you get a head start on making your chart look great and matching the other information you will be putting with it. Styles help you by applying predefined color sets, backgrounds, and special effects. Chart layouts define what will show on the chart, including the title, the labels, and the legend. Layouts also give you a head start on where each of these items will appear.

Chart Styles

There are 48 chart styles for regular pie charts, and there are eight sets of colors that can be applied. For each set of colors, there are six sets of other formatting. Each set combines a background, a pie shape effect, and a line color with the color set to make up a distinct style (see Figure 4-11).

As with the other chart types, 48 styles don't go very far in the real world. At a minimum, you are going to need to target the colors to match the ones used in the rest of your materials. If you have predefined colors for the items you are charting (for example, company standard colors or packaging colors for a product), then use those colors for your slice colors. If you don't have

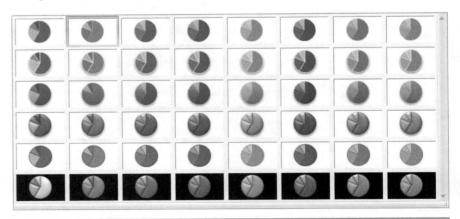

Figure 4-11   Available chart styles for pie charts

MEMO

Some of the effects don't work the way you would expect for pie charts. You cannot, for example, set a pie slice to have a 3-D effect. Such effects need to be added by setting the chart type to a 3-D chart. If you turn on a shadow, it may or may not show. This is because the shadows are applied from one side to the other. By the very nature of a pie chart, the rest of the chart may hide part of your shadow.

predefined colors, be careful what colors you use for the shapes. It is always better to be conservative in your color choices than to be bold. Shades of the same color are safer choices than puce, hot pink, and bright blue. If you thought bad color choices looked interesting in a bar or column chart, wait until you see what the colors do when next to each other in a pie chart.

Beyond the color choices, you can also change the look of each slice of the pie. Be careful with this. In general, applying an effect to a slice can make it stand out nicely from the other slices. It is easy to go too far and have them all formatted differently—that doesn't look professional.

If you do want to use effects to set off your slices, try turning on the soft shadows. It gives the effect of having exploded out the pie slices but without moving the slices. Do not apply the soft shadow to just one slice, however: It will shrink the whole slice and make it appear to be a different size than the rest of the slices. Combining the soft shadow with a glow gives an interesting effect too. I wouldn't recommend using it frequently, but it is a way to highlight a specific slice.

The other effect I find quite useful is the bevels. By beveling the edges of your slices, your chart becomes more professional-looking. A simple bevel application to the pieces in your chart will make it stand out from all the other charts and make you look really good.

Finally, about the backgrounds... Use the ones that come in the color sets. Use the darker ones when presenting so that the chart pops, and use the lighter ones when printing to save ink or toner. If you are going to pick a background color other than one of the defaults, make sure that it coordinates with the slice colors and that all of the slice colors show up against it.

Chart Layouts

There are seven chart layouts for regular pie charts (see Figure 4-12). These define where the title goes, where the labels go, and where the legend goes.

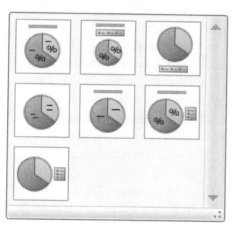

Figure 4-12   Available chart layouts for pie charts

MEMO

There are two additional layouts that apply only to the bar of pie and pie of pie charts. Those will be covered at the end of the chapter when these chart types are discussed.

When trying to decide which chart style to use, start by considering what should be seen about the data. For pie charts, I prefer to have data labels attached to the slices rather than in a separate legend. It makes it easier to see what slice represents which data. I always put a title on my charts, so I seldom use the title-less layouts. The final layout decision is whether you want to show the values as numbers, percentages, or not show them at all.

No matter which chart style you are using, you will need to do some alterations to the chart after you apply the style. The default chart layouts have a few quirks you will want to correct.

You are likely to find that you want to enlarge the size of the pie chart itself. The larger the chart on the screen, the better it will print or import into other tools. To stretch the pie chart, click the chart and select the plot area. (You can do this via Chart Tools | Layout | Current Selection as well.) Stretch the lower-right corner out and down to the edge of the screen. Then stretch the upper-left corner out and up to just below the title of the chart. By stretching from the corners, you ensure that the chart remains correctly proportioned without going over the top of other elements.

If the labels or the values on the pie slices are shown on the slices, the font size for them will need to be increased. For some reason, the pie charts made in Excel 2007 have a default font size of 10 point. This is not nearly big enough for most chart usage. To change the font size, click one of the labels and use Home | Font Size to increase the size. Go as large as you can without the labels running over the edge of the slice.

If you have a large number of slices in your pie, the labels may not fit nicely within the slices. In this case, you will want to move them outside of the slices. Click a label to select it, and then right-click to bring up the Format Labels dialog. Here you can adjust your labels so that they look exactly how you desire.

First choice: Decide what you want to show for the labels. Do you want the label name, the value, the percentage, or none of these? If the labels don't fit within the slice, or if you set the labels to appear outside of the slices, do you want lines leading back to the slices? As you make the layout choices for your

THE EASY WAY

Want some of the data labels in one place and the others in another place? Format the full set of labels the way you want most of them. Then select each of the other labels, and drag them to where you want them. For any of the labels that you move off the slice, leader lines will show if you have selected that check box.

labels, check or uncheck the appropriate box. As always with a format dialog, you will see each change immediately and can decide if it is the right one for this data.

Second choice: Decide where you want the labels to sit on the chart. This is where the leader lines come into play. Do you want the labels to sit on the slices or off the slices? Outside the end of your slices is generally a good look. Inside the slices at the center of the pie usually isn't.

Finally: Decide whether you want the data label to be on one line or more than one line and what you want for a delimiter. Play around with the choices here: Some charts you will want one way, while others you will want another. One thing to know for sure: If your labels are near your pie slices instead of in a legend, your chart will look cleaner if you uncheck Include Legend Key in Label. This option turns on the little box of color that shows which label goes with which slice. If your labels are on the slices, these boxes will not show. If they are off the slices, it will be clearer if you use leader lines than the little color swatch boxes.

2-D vs. 3-D Charts

In addition to the 2-D pie charts used so far in this chapter, there are two other chart types: the regular 3-D pie and the exploded 3-D pie. In a pie chart, either the entire chart is turned on an axis or none of it is. That makes the 3-D charts easier to work with, but it also limits what can be done with them.

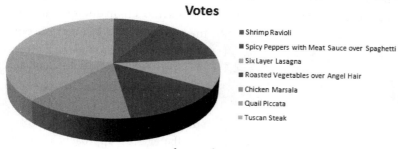

Figure 4-13 Original chart moved to 3-D

Whether exploded or not, 3-D pie charts do not change how the data is graphed. Unlike the other 3-D charts, where the data is actually plotted along a third axis, in this case, adding the third dimension does nothing more than add depth to the circle. Basically, by moving into the third dimension, you lay the pie down instead of looking at it face-on (see Figure 4-13).

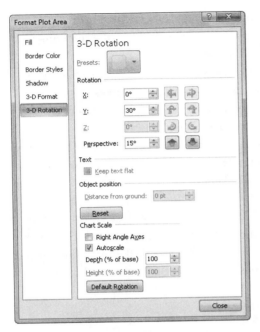

In fact, as Figure 4-13 shows, the difference between a 2-D pie and a 3-D pie is slight. In this chart, the extra dimension adds a bit of depth to the chart, but the depth doesn't even show in all of the pieces.

By moving into the third dimension, you can adjust how much tilt is applied and where the light is coming from. You can also adjust the apparent material used to create the slices. All of these changes are made via the 3-D options area of the Format Plot Area dialog (see Figure 4-14). To get to the options, select the plot area, right-click, and bring up the Format dialog. Click 3-D Rotation.

To adjust how flat the bottom of the disc is, change the value for the rotation around the y axis. The lower this number, the closer the disc is to lying on its back. The higher the number, the closer the disc is to standing on edge. Standing the disc fully on its edge in effect changes it back to a 2-D pie.

Figure 4-14 Format Plot Area dialog – 3-D Rotation options

Changing the rotation around the x axis spins the disc. This is the same as changing the rotation angle of the first slice of the pie. Changing the perspective value does the same as changing the rotation around the y axis, but stretches the shape of the pie so that it appears that the back of the pie is farther away than the front. If the perspective is set to a high enough number, the base of the pie will become out-of-round and taper towards a point.

Be careful when playing with the rotation values for pie charts. As the rotation value around the y axis gets smaller, the disc becomes flatter and flatter. As it approaches 0, you

Votes

- Shrimp Ravioli
- Spicy Peppers with Meat Sauce over Spaghetti
- Six Layer Lasagna
- Roasted Vegetables over Angel Hair
- Chicken Marsala
- Quail Piccata
- Tuscan Steak

Figure 4-15 Over-rotated 3-D pie chart

no longer see a pie chart; you instead see just the edge of the slices at the bottom of the pie, as shown in Figure 4-15.

MEMO

See the button labeled Default Rotation? You would hope that clicking that button would change the rotation back to the default values. It doesn't. Instead, it makes the current settings the default values for this chart. From that point on, if you click the Reset button, the chart will revert to these settings instead of the original ones. What's worse is that the new default applies to all charts of this type within this file.

THE EASY WAY

Besides looking better, another reason to use 3-D charts is because they can take up less space on the page or slide. Because the chart is tilted into the third dimension, the chart is shorter. This is only true for pie charts, not for the other charts discussed in this book.

What about an exploded 3-D pie chart? What does it look like? Pretty much what you would expect. The pieces are moved out from center, just as they are on the 2-D chart. One interesting effect of exploding a 3-D chart with the perspective turned up is that the pieces automatically seem to curve from the center down to the edge, as shown in Figure 4-16.

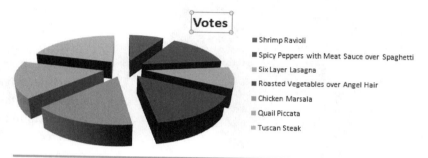

Figure 4-16   Exploded 3-D pie chart with perspective turned up

Formatting Individual Pie Pieces

All these color choices are nice enough, but a picture speaks much clearer than a colored segment. If each pie piece had a picture of the recipe that was being voted on, the chart story would have an immediate impact. The process for adding the pictures to the slices is familiar, but there are two things to watch out for when using pictures in pie slices.

Because slices are not regular shapes, Excel is going to take a part of your picture and use it to create the fill. You can use the offset values to change where the picture sits in the shape, but you still have to be careful with how it is done.

Select the green piece of the pie (the Lasagna slice) and bring up the Format dialog. Go to the Fill section. Change the selection to Picture or Texture Fill. If you have selected a picture or texture fill in the past for any item in Office, that picture will show as the default fill. To pick a different fill, click the Clip Art button.

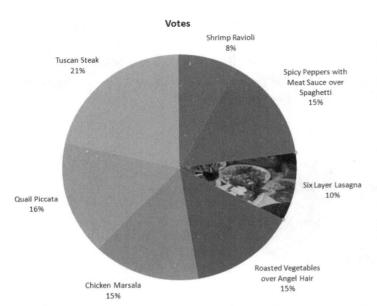

Votes

Shrimp Ravioli
8%

Tuscan Steak
21%

Spicy Peppers with
Meat Sauce over
Spaghetti
15%

Six Layer Lasagna
10%

Quail Piccata
16%

Roasted Vegetables
over Angel Hair
15%

Chicken Marsala
15%

Figure 4-17   Lasagna picture fill for pie slice

MEMO

If you prefer to use a picture from your own collection, click the File button and navigate to the picture from there. Once the picture is inserted, the rest of this procedure works just the same as with the clip art.

The Select Picture dialog will appear. Check the box to ensure Office Online art is searched as well, and then search for Lasagna. One of the results will be a photograph of a lasagna serving. Select that picture and click OK. The lasagna picture will appear in your slice (see Figure 4-17).

The picture appears with the center of the picture at the center of the slice. Since the lasagna is what needs to be highlighted, the picture needs to be moved around so that the lasagna is centered. You would hope that you could use the Stretch options to move the picture around. Unfortunately, this doesn't work quite the way you might think. Instead of moving the picture within the area of the slice, the offsets squeeze the picture in from top, bottom, left, or right. This gives a rather squished appearance to drawings and adds white space around the photographs. Neither of these results is professional-looking.

All is not lost, though. Instead of changing the picture, change the graph. First, check the box for tile picture. In some cases, this will shift the picture over enough to center the important part of it. If it doesn't shift far enough, move to the Series Options section of the Format Data Point dialog and try rotating the graph. In this case, tiling the picture and rotating the graph 30 degrees gives a much nicer result (see Figure 4-18).

Another solution to the alignment problem with picture fills is to use a plain picture with no background. Select the Spicy Peppers slice. Again, bring up the Select Picture dialog to find a fill for the slice. This time, search for Peppers.

Votes

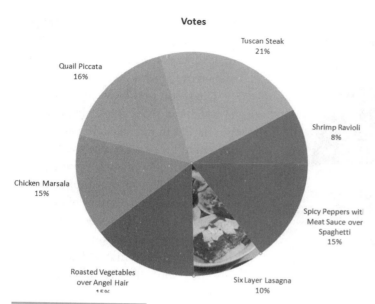

Figure 4-18   Better lasagna picture fill for pie slice

MEMO

While this process works if you are only adding one picture or graphic, you may not be able to get all the pictures to line up if you are using multiple pictures. In this case, save the clip art piece to your hard drive and use a graphics editor to adjust what is in the center of the picture.

One of the items found will be a set of spicy red peppers on a white background. Select this picture and insert it into the graph, as shown in Figure 4-19.

Notice that this time the picture is off towards the center of the graph. Set the left offset to 30 by either typing the number or using the arrows. Set the bottom offset to 20. When both adjustments are made, the peppers will have moved to the center of the slice.

Votes

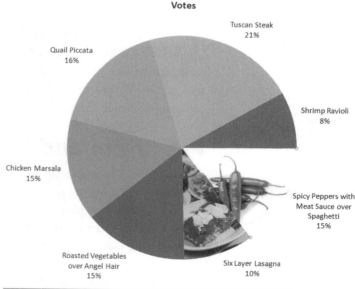

Figure 4-19   Peppers picture fill for pie slice

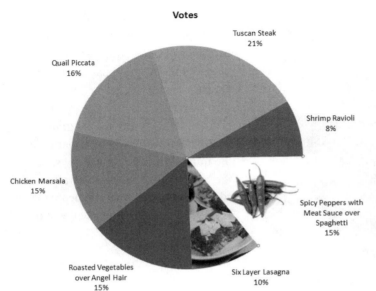

Votes

Tuscan Steak
21%

Quail Piccata
16%

Shrimp Ravioli
8%

Chicken Marsala
15%

Spicy Peppers with
Meat Sauce over
Spaghetti
15%

Roasted Vegetables
over Angel Hair
15%

Six Layer Lasagna
10%

Figure 4-20   Better peppers picture fill for pie slice

Because the background of the pepper picture is white, the blank fill for the offset area doesn't cause a problem, as shown in Figure 4-20.

The second problem you need to watch out for is more obvious, but harder to fix. Select the slice for Quail Picatta. Change the fill on the shape to Gradient. Notice that the gradient that is applied is not the orange gradient? This is because the default gradient is the last one you used. If you want to have the gradient match your chosen pie slice, you will need to build the gradient by hand.

Click the drop-down arrow for the color. Select the palest orange. This will change the color for the first gradient stop to light orange. Click the drop-down arrow for the stop, and change it from Stop 1 to Stop 2. Change the color for this stop to the middle orange in the color chart. Repeat for Stop 3, selecting the darkest orange. You now have a nice gradient fill that matches your original color choice.

Pie of Pie and Bar of Pie Charts

Another way to approach the problem of too many slices for a pie chart is to create either a pie of pie or bar of pie chart. In these charts, several of the smaller pieces of the pie are automatically grouped together in one slice. Then, a second chart is made from those slices and connected to the slice that was grouped.

Let's look at a separate set of data from the restaurant to see what you would use these two charts for. At the same time that the menu survey was

Votes

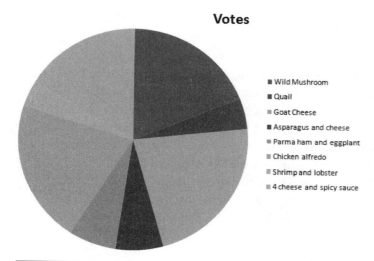

- Wild Mushroom
- Quail
- Goat Cheese
- Asparagus and cheese
- Parma ham and eggplant
- Chicken alfredo
- Shrimp and lobster
- 4 cheese and spicy sauce

Figure 4-21   Pizza voting chart

being done, the restaurant was trying eight new toppings. The plan was to add five of these toppings to the menu. While the pie chart from the results clearly showed the top four results, the fifth result was hard to see (see Figure 4-21).

You could take the data for this graph and rearrange it by hand so that it is clearer which of the toppings gets added. However, there is a better way.

While viewing the chart, click the Chart Tools | Design | Change Chart Type button. Change the type to Pie of Pie.

Not much better at first glance, is it? But here is where the power of these two chart types comes in. By default, the slices moved to the secondary graph are the last three positions in the circle. But you can also determine which slices are going over by value, percentage, or a custom setting.

When you choose Value, you then must determine the maximum value to go into the second graph. Setting the maximum value to 10 moves the bottom three choices to the new graph. The percentage split works the same way. Select Percentage, set the split value to 15 percent, and the charts are split four and four (see Figure 4-22).

Votes

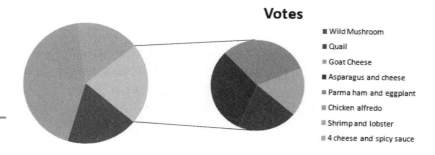

- Wild Mushroom
- Quail
- Goat Cheese
- Asparagus and cheese
- Parma ham and eggplant
- Chicken alfredo
- Shrimp and lobster
- 4 cheese and spicy sauce

Figure 4-22   Pizza voting chart as pie of pie

What about custom? When you select Custom, you can choose data point by data point which chart will contain that point. To see this, change Split Series by to Custom. Click any of the values in one chart. Use the Point Belongs To drop-down list to move it to the other chart. Notice the power it gives you to rearrange your data to tell you more about the results.

There are three other ways you can customize the secondary chart. Of these, the most useful is the Second Plot Size. Adjusting this slider makes the secondary chart bigger or smaller. The more points you chart on the secondary chart, the larger you should make it for readability.

What, then, is a bar of pie chart? Instead of the second chart being a pie chart, the second chart is a bar chart. It works just the same, but offers a different perspective on the results.

Creating and Formatting a Basic Area Chart

Area charts are a combination of line charts (discussed in Chapter 3) and pie charts (discussed in Chapter 4). Line charts summarize trends in data series across categories; in most cases, those categories are time periods, such as days, months, or years. Pie charts, by contrast, display how much each category of data contributes to the total within a single data series. Area charts summarize how the contributions of categories of data have changed over time. For example, you could create a chart summarizing how many customer support calls five products have generated for each month over the past year.

In this chapter you will learn how to create an area chart from data, identify the basic parts of an area chart (such as the one shown in Figure 5-1), format your chart using built-in styles and layouts, and create and rotate a 3-D area chart.

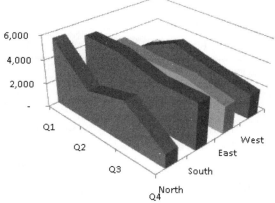

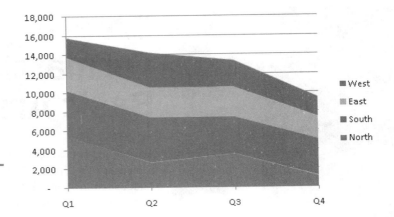

Figure 5-1   A stacked area chart indicates the trend of how much each data series contributes to the whole.

Creating an Area Chart from Data

Table 5-1 contains a data set that can be summarized using an area chart or a line chart, but, because of the multiple data series within the set, cannot be summarized using a pie chart.

	Q1	Q2	Q3	Q4
North	4,823	4,767	3,905	3,876
South	2,105	1,683	1,414	2,682
East	672	810	1,129	1,031
West	450	600	573	801

Table 5-1   Sample Data That Can Be Summarized Using an Area Chart

MEMO

If one or more of your data series is mostly or completely obscured in an area chart, you should strongly consider summarizing your data using a line chart.

The data in Table 5-1 is laid out in *cross-tabular* format, where each cell in the table occurs at the intersection of two header values (e.g., the value 450 occurs at the intersection of the West row and the Q1 column). This dual categorization of the data in the table enables Excel to create a chart that summarizes both the magnitude of each value and how the values trend across the set's categories.

MEMO

A 100% stacked area chart, like a pie chart, indicates how significantly each data series contributes to the whole, but a pie chart only summarizes a single data series. You should create a 100% stacked area chart instead of a pie chart when your data is stored in a cross-tab format and contains more than one data series.

Types of Area Charts

Excel 2007 enables you to create three basic types of area chart: a regular *area chart*, a *stacked area chart*, and a *100% stacked area chart* (plus a 3-D variation of each basic subtype). Which subtype you choose depends on how you want to summarize your data.

A regular area chart displays each data series as a shape within the chart and enables the viewer to compare visually the relative magnitude of the values in each series. The top of each shape represents the values in the series, and the shape extends down to the horizontal axis. Depending on the order in which Excel plots your data series in the chart, series that contain larger values can completely obscure series that contain smaller values. Figure 5-2 shows an area chart where each value in a data series is smaller than the values in the series plotted behind it in the chart.

A stacked area chart, such as the chart shown at the beginning of this chapter in Figure 5-1, summarizes the trend of how much each data set contributes to the total value of each series' categories. The top border of the uppermost data series indicates the total for each category. A 100% stacked area chart, such as the one shown in Figure 5-3, summarizes the trend of what percentage each category of data contributes to the total value for that category.

75

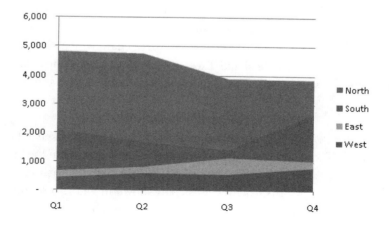

Figure 5-2   No data series in this chart completely obscures the values in another data series.

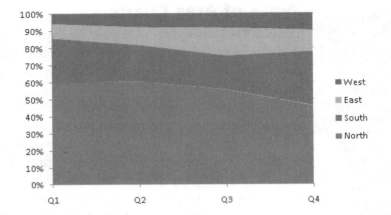

Figure 5-3   Stacked area charts display all data to emphasize how each data series contributes to the overall totals.

How Excel Plots Your Data in Each Chart Subtype

The order in which your data occurs in the data set affects how Excel creates your area chart. How the data series' order affects your charts changes by the area chart subtype you choose to create. In a 2-D area chart, Excel assigns the data set's column headers to the horizontal axis and the row headers to the legend (indicating that they represent individual data series). Excel then adds the data by placing the topmost data row in the back of the chart and adds each subsequent row in front of the preceding row.

When you create a 3-D area chart, which displays each data series as a separate shape, Excel reverses the order of the data series in the chart. Rather than display the topmost data series in back and add subsequent series in front of existing data, Excel adds the topmost series to the front of the chart and adds subsequent series behind it.

In 2-D stacked area charts and 100% stacked area charts, as shown in Figure 5-4, Excel plots the first row of data on the bottom of the chart and places each subsequent row on top of the existing data in the chart.

To create the area chart shown in Figure 5-4, you will create a 2-D area chart and then change the chart's type.

MEMO

Area charts summarize data trends, so if your data set has a time element, such as months, quarters, or years, you should strongly consider organizing those time-related values on the horizontal (category) axis. If your time-related data elements appear on the vertical axis, click Chart Tools | Design | Switch Row/ Column Data to plot the time data on the horizontal axis.

1. Open the Excel file Chap05Table.xlsx, and display the 2006 worksheet, which contains quarterly call data for a fictitious company's four regional call centers during the calendar year 2006.

2. In the range A1:E5, click any cell that contains data.

3. On the Insert tab of the ribbon, in the Charts group, click Area, and then click the first chart subtype under the 2-D Area header.

4. Click Chart Tools | Design | Change Chart Type to display the Change Chart Type dialog. In the Area group of the dialog, click the third chart subtype from the left, the 100% Stacked Area subtype, and then click OK to close the dialog.

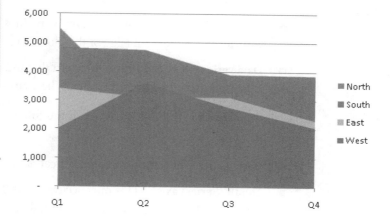

Figure 5-4   A 2-D area chart orders data series to reflect the series' order in your worksheet.

Basic Parts of an Area Chart

Excel 2007 charts consist of distinct elements that you can format independently. To select a chart element, click Chart Tools | Layout, and then, in the Current Selection group on the ribbon, click the Chart Elements list box's down arrow and select the desired element from the list that appears. You can then use the tools on the ribbon to format the selected element.

In a 2-D area chart, you can format the following elements:

- **Chart area** This is the part of the chart that contains the legend, chart title, and axis titles.

- **Horizontal (Category) axis** This displays the categories denoted by the data set's column headers.

- **Legend** This lists the data series in the chart (denoted by the data set's row headers).

- **Plot area** This contains the shapes summarizing each data series.

- **Vertical (Value) axis** This displays numeric values indicating the total of the values in the chart's data series.

- **Vertical (Value) axis gridlines** These are lines extending from the vertical axis to the right edge of the plot area.

- **Data series** Shapes within the chart that indicate the magnitude of values contained within each row of the chart's data set.

3-D area charts contain some or all of the following additional chart elements:

- **Back wall** This represents the vertical plane behind the plot area.

- **Depth (Series) axis** This only occurs in the 3-D area chart. It represents the values displayed to the right of each data series. The Depth (Series) axis contains the same values as the chart's legend.

- **Floor** This represents the horizontal plane below the chart's plot area.

- **Side wall** This represents the vertical plane that extends from the vertical axis to the back wall.

- **Walls** These represent both the chart's back wall and side wall.

Formatting Your Chart Using Built-in Styles and Layouts

Office 2007 includes many new formatting capabilities, including the ability to use many more colors and designs when creating charts in Excel. The built-in styles and layouts, which control the appearance and design of your charts, respectively, enable you to select a look that meets your needs. Of course, if no pre-built style or layout is exactly right, you can assign your chart a design that you can modify with a minimum of effort to create the look you want.

Chart Styles

You can find Excel 2007's built-in chart styles by clicking the chart you want to format and then, on the Design contextual tab, clicking the Chart Styles gallery's More button to display the available styles. Some of the built-in styles use shades of a single color, such as blue or green, to distinguish data series. Other styles, such as the one shown in Figure 5-5, set each series apart by using different fill colors.

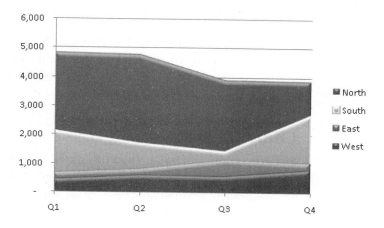

Figure 5-5   Select the chart style that displays your data most effectively.

To create the chart shown in Figure 5-5, you will display the Chart Styles gallery, select a style, and add a 2-point white border to one of the chart's data series.

1. Open the Excel file Chap05StylesAndLayout.xlsx, and display the 2006 worksheet, which contains a chart summarizing quarterly call data for a fictitious company's four regional call centers during the calendar year 2006.

2. Click the chart, and then click Chart Tools | Design to display the Design contextual tab.

3. In the Chart Styles group, click the Chart Styles gallery's More button, which appears at the lower-right corner of the gallery, and then click Style 25, which renders the chart's data series using varying shades of gray and gives each series area a beveled edge.

4. Click Chart Tools | Format, and then, in the Current Selection group, click the Chart Elements list box's down arrow, and click Series "South." In the same group, click the Format Selection button to display the Format Data Series dialog.

5. In the Categories panel, click Border Color, select the Solid Line option, click the Color button, and click the White, Background 1 square at the upper-left corner of the color palette.

6. In the Categories panel, click Border Styles, and then use the Width spin control to set the border line's width to 2 pt. Click Close to close the Format Data Series dialog. Click any spot in the chart's chart area to display the new border line without the selection highlight.

Chart Layouts

Just as you can format your chart using a built-in chart style, you can also select from one of several built-in chart layouts. These layouts control the appearance and position of the chart's legend, chart title, axis titles, gridlines, and so on. One example of a built-in chart layout appears in Figure 5-6.

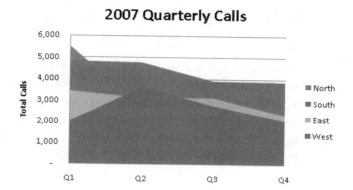

Figure 5-6   Each built-in chart layout highlights different chart elements.

You can fine-tune your chart's layout by clicking the chart and using the controls on the Layout contextual tab.

To create the chart shown in Figure 5-6, you will display the Chart Tools | Design contextual tab, select a chart layout, and fill in the chart's title and vertical axis title.

1. Open the Excel file Chap05StylesAndLayout.xlsx, and display the 2007 worksheet, which contains a chart summarizing quarterly call data for a fictitious company's four regional call centers during the calendar year 2007.

2. Click the chart, and then click Chart Tools | Design to display the Design contextual tab.

3. In the Chart Layouts group, click the group's More button, which appears at the lower-right corner of the layout gallery, and click the first layout on the first row (the tooltip "Layout 1" appears when you hover your mouse pointer over this button).

4. Click the Chart Title text box, select the text in the box, and type **2007 Quarterly Calls**.

5. On the vertical axis, click the Axis Title text box, select the text in the box, and type **Total Calls**.

Creating and Rotating a 3-D Area Chart

With the exception of the 3-D area chart, which plots individual data series in a 3-D chart, none of the "3-D" area chart subtypes are truly 3-D charts. Why? Because the cross-tab data sets used to create an area chart contain no data that can be used to provide depth or size to the chart's shapes. All of the values are used to define the height and width of the shapes representing the chart's data series. Rather than misusing the existing data, Excel applies consistent 3-D formatting to the chart to imply a third dimension where there is none.

Creating a 3-D area chart is simply a matter of selecting one of the 3-D area chart subtypes when you make the chart or change its type. If you'd like to rotate your chart, perhaps to better reveal the shape summarizing your data series, you can rotate the chart along the x axis, along the y axis, or by changing your perspective.

There are three axes by which you can rotate a 3-D object: the x (horizontal), y (vertical), and z (proximity) axes. One good way to visualize these axes and the effect of changing perspective is by placing an empty coffee cup on your desk with the mouth up and the handle to your right. Now, if you

- Rotate the cup so the mouth is still up but the handle is on the left, you have rotated the cup in the x (horizontal) axis

- Rotate the cup so the handle is still on your left but the cup is now mouth-down, you have rotated the cup in the y (vertical) axis

- Push the cup away from you, you have shifted the cup in the z (proximity) axis

- Stand up from your chair (or sit down if you were standing), you have changed your perspective

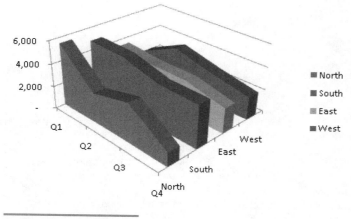

Figure 5-7   A 3-D rotated
area chart

The z (proximity) axis doesn't really apply to 3-D charts—you can simulate shifting a chart away from you or toward you by making it smaller or larger—so the 3-D Rotation page of the Format Chart Area dialog just lets you change the chart's x axis rotation, y axis rotation, and Perspective properties. You could, for example, create the chart displayed in Figure 5-7.

To create the chart shown in Figure 5-7, you will create a 3-D area chart, display the 3-D Rotation page of the Format Chart Area dialog, and change the chart's 3-D formatting.

1. Open the Excel file Chap05AreaChartIn3D.xlsx, and display the 2007 worksheet, which contains a chart summarizing quarterly call data for a fictitious company's four regional call centers during the calendar year 2007.

2. In the cell range A1:E5, click any cell that contains data, and then click the Insert tab. In the Charts group, click the Area button, and then click the 3-D Area chart subtype (the first subtype in the 3-D Area group of chart subtypes).

3. Click Chart Tools | Layout and then, in the Background group, click 3-D Rotation to display the 3-D Rotation page of the Format Chart Area dialog.

4. In the Rotation section of the dialog, type **45** in the X box, type **30** in the Y box, and type **20** in the Perspective box. Click the Close button to close the dialog.

GAPS IN YOUR DATA AND CHARTS

Excel 2007 handles blank cells in data sets inconsistently, depending on the type of area chart you create. When you create any area chart subtype except for the basic 2-D area chart, blank cells in your data series will be treated as having zero values in those positions. One example of a chart that correctly handles blank cells appears in Figure 5-8.

When you create a 2-D area chart from the same data series, however, Excel doesn't plot all (or, in some cases, any) of the data series' values. What appears to be happening is that Excel's 2-D area chart creation routine doesn't have built-in logic to handle blank cells. Every other area chart subtype, however, does have that built-in logic. For example, creating a stacked area chart requires Excel to calculate the total of the values in each of the data set's columns and draw the chart's regions to reflect those values.

The same considerations hold true for the 100% stacked area chart subtype.

The 3-D area chart subtype, an example of which appears in Figure 5-8, is superficially similar to the 2-D area chart subtype, but it displays each of the data series' rows as a separate column in the chart. Excel 2007 creates the 3-D area chart subtype correctly even if the data set contains blank cells, so it appears that routine contains logic to handle blank values.

If your data set contains any blank cells, you can type a zero (or, as it turns out, a non-numerical value, such as the word *cat* or *dog*) in those cells to create the area chart correctly. If, for any reason, you can't edit the cells from which you create the chart and are required to summarize your data in a 2-D area chart, create any area chart subtype, except for a 2-D area chart, and then change the chart's type to a 2-D area chart to ensure that Excel 2007 displays your data accurately.

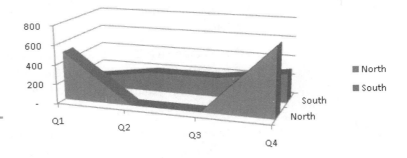

Figure 5-8 In this area chart, Excel substitutes zero values for blank cells.

Creating and Formatting a Scatter Chart

Scatter (XY) charts summarize two data series where both the horizontal and vertical axes contain values that Excel uses to determine where to plot each data point in the body of the chart. Scatter charts are most useful for plotting financial and scientific data. For example, you could record the temperature and humidity at a particular time over a period of months or years, and plot the data on a scatter chart to help you discover whether there is any relation between the two values. In the financial world, you could measure a company's net revenue for a quarter and note how much the company's stock gained or lost value on the day the results were announced.

In this chapter you will learn how to create a scatter chart (such as the chart displayed in Figure 6-1), format your charts by hand, and add trend lines to your charts.

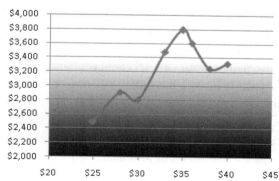

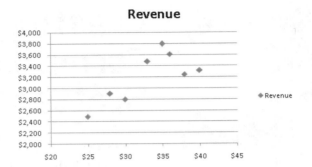

Figure 6-1   A sample scatter chart

Creating a Scatter Chart from Data

As the chart and data set displayed in Figure 6-1 demonstrates, you create a scatter chart from a two-column data source, where both columns contain numerical values. If you have a two-column data source where one of the rows contains categories of information, such as companies or products, you should summarize your data using a column or bar chart. If your data source contains a column of time values, such as years, you should strongly consider creating a line chart that plots the time values on the horizontal axis.

Scatter charts map the value pairs in the data set by placing markers in the body of the chart to indicate the intersection of the two values. You can also add lines to connect the markers and indicate trends within the data, but which chart subtype you choose depends on the data with which you create the scatter chart. For example, in a chart mapping temperature and humidity measurements, each marker would represent both the temperature and humidity values captured during each measurement. If your data set could contain multiple examples of the same value, such as finding the same temperature in two or more measurements, you should create a scatter chart using only data markers.

On the other hand, if you know your data set contains a single occurrence of each temperature, selecting a scatter chart subtype that draws lines between the markers could illustrate a pattern or trend in your data. Figure 6-2 shows one such chart.

MEMO

If you'd like to examine the trends found in a data set more carefully, you should create a trend line that reflects how the values on the vertical axis relate to the values on the horizontal axis. For more information on adding trend lines to a chart, see the "Trend Lines and Scatter Charts" section at the end of this chapter.

86

Figure 6-2 A scatter chart where the line helps you interpret the chart's data

To create the scatter chart shown in Figure 6-2, you will create a scatter chart that summarizes your data using markers and then change the chart to another scatter chart subtype that also includes lines.

1. Open the Excel 2007 file Chap06Table.xlsx. The PriceCheck worksheet contains a table of price and revenue data from a fictitious company's test sales of a product at varying price points.

2. Click any cell in the table, click Insert | Scatter, and then click the first scatter chart subtype. The tooltip *Scatter with only Markers* appears when you hover the mouse pointer over the correct chart subtype.

3. Click the chart and then, if necessary, click Chart Tools | Design | Change Chart Type to display the Change Chart Type dialog. In the list of chart subtypes, click the second subtype from the left under the X Y (Scatter) category header. The tooltip *Scatter with Smooth Lines and Markers* appears when you hover the mouse pointer over the correct chart subtype.

4. Click OK to dismiss the dialog.

Formatting Your Chart by Hand

The basic scatter charts that Excel creates display your data effectively, but the standard blue markers and lines on a white background might not give you the look you want. You can change the formatting of any element in your chart by displaying the dialog that contains controls specific to the currently selected chart element.

Format the Plot Area

A scatter chart's plot area contains the data displayed, or *plotted*, in the body of the chart. When you create a scatter chart, the default chart style includes a borderless white plot area. If you want to change the plot area's formatting, you can change the background, or *fill*, so that it is a solid color, gradient, picture, or texture.

A *gradient* is a gradual transition between colors. The gradient shown in Figure 6-3 starts with pure white at the top and adds more black until the fill color changes to pure black at the bottom of the plot area.

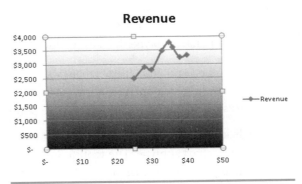

Figure 6-3   This gradient changes evenly from white at the top to black at the bottom.

To add a gradient fill pattern to your chart's plot area, you can right-click the plot area and click Format Plot Area to display the dialog of the same name. On the Fill page of the dialog, which appears by default, select the Gradient Fill option to display the controls you'll use to define your gradient. Those options appear in Figure 6-4.

Excel 2007 comes with a series of predefined gradient fill patterns; to display them, click the Preset Colors button. Clicking any of the patterns in the palette applies that pattern to the chart's plot area and displays the gradient's properties in the Gradient Stops section of the dialog.

88

MEMO

The gradient fill options for type, direction, and angle all affect your fill pattern, but there are too many combinations to fit in this chapter. Using the instructions in this section, experiment with different fill patterns to get a feel for each setting's effects.

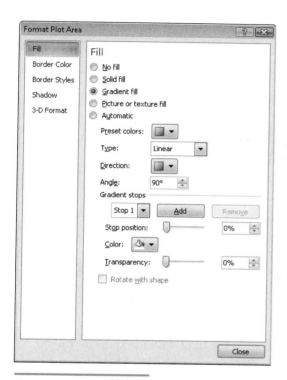

Figure 6-4   Use the Format Plot Area dialog to change your plot area's fill pattern.

A gradient stop defines the color Excel applies to a portion of a chart element (in this case, the plot area). As an example, consider the gradient fill shown in Figure 6-5. This gradient, which is of the Linear Up type, consists of a white fill for the top 35 percent of the plot area, followed by a gradual transition from that 35 percent mark to a 100 percent black fill at the bottom. The pattern is made up of two gradient stops, the first of which appears in the Gradient Stops section of the Format Plot Area dialog.

To create the chart in Figure 6-5, you will edit an existing gradient fill by removing a gradient stop and changing the remaining two stops so that the top 35 percent of the plot area is pure white and then gradually changes to a pure black field at the bottom of the plot area.

1. Open the Excel 2007 file Chap06Format.xlsx. The PlotArea worksheet contains a chart that summarizes how changing a product's price in several test markets affected total sales revenue in those markets.

2. Right-click any spot in the chart's plot area, and then click Format Plot Area to display the dialog of the same name. If necessary, on the Fill page of the dialog, select the Gradient Fill option.

3. Click the Direction button, and then click the second item on the top row of the palette. The tooltip *Linear Down* appears when you hover the mouse pointer over that item.

4. In the Gradient Stops section of the dialog, click the down arrow at the right edge of the Stops list box, which currently displays the text Stop 1. Click Stop 3, and then click the Remove button. The Stops list box now displays Stop 2.

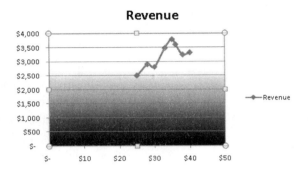

Figure 6-5 This chart's fill uses gradient stops to create a more complex pattern.

5. Drag the Stop Position slider all the way to the right end of the slider bar so that the value in the Stop Position spin control to the right of the slider reads 100%. Click the Color button, and click the Black, Text 1 square, which is in the second position from the left on the top row.

6. Click the down arrow at the right edge of the Stops list box, which currently displays the text Stop 2, and click Stop 1.

7. Drag the Stop Position slider to the right until the spin control to the right of the slider bar contains the value 35%. Then click the Color button, and, from the palette that appears, click the White, Background 1 square at the top right of the palette. Click the Close button to dismiss the dialog.

MEMO

Excel changes the bottom two horizontal grid lines from black to a medium gray when the black lines would not stand out against the fill color in that part of the plot area.

Format the Axis

When you create a scatter chart, Excel analyzes the data used to create the chart and adds those values to the chart's horizontal and vertical axes. By default, Excel starts each axis either at zero or at the lowest value in the series. If your data falls within a relatively small range, you might find the data markers and lines crowded into one tiny section of your chart. You can change how Excel plots your data by resizing the chart or by changing the starting and ending values on the chart's axes.

If you want to change the values on an axis, right-click any value on the axis, and click Format Axis to display the Format Axis dialog. On the Axis Options page of the dialog, you can change the lowest and highest values on the axis by using the Minimum and Maximum controls. To change the minimum value displayed on an axis, select the Minimum control row's Fixed option, and type the desired value in the text box located to the right. You can then change the maximum value by following the same steps, this time using the controls on the Maximum control row. A chart with modified axis values appears in Figure 6-6.

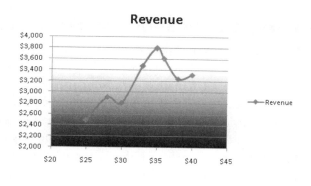

Figure 6-6   Changing a chart's axis values helps you focus on your data.

To create the chart in Figure 6-6, you will display the Format Axis dialog and change the minimum values on both the horizontal and vertical axes.

1. Open the Excel 2007 file Chap06Format.xlsx. The Axis worksheet contains a chart that summarizes how changing a product's price in several test markets affected total sales revenue in those markets.

2. Right-click any value on the vertical axis, and click Format Axis to display the Format Axis dialog.

3. At the top of the Axis Options page of the dialog, in the Minimum control row, select the Fixed option. In the text box located to the right, type the value **2000**.

4. In the chart, click any value on the horizontal axis to change the Format Axis dialog's contents to reflect the horizontal axis' settings. (If you pressed ENTER after you typed the value into the text box, the

MEMO

Be aware that changing a chart's axis values can change how viewers will interpret your chart's data. Make certain your changes don't mislead your audience.

91

Format Axis dialog disappeared. If that happened, right-click the horizontal axis and click Format Axis to bring it back.)

5. At the top of the Axis Options page of the dialog, in the Minimum control row, select the Fixed option. In the text box located to the right, type the value **20**. Click Close to dismiss the dialog box.

Format Data Series Markers and Lines

Which markers you choose to represent your data is largely a matter of taste. If you create a small chart, you should reduce the size of the data markers so your viewers can more easily distinguish between them. Similarly, if your chart contains many data points, you should consider using smaller markers so the individual data points don't obscure their neighbors.

Many of the same considerations come into play when you format the lines on your scatter chart. If the data trends are more important than the individual values, you can make the lines thicker and more brightly colored than the data markers. If the trends are important, but not as important as the individual data points, you should format the chart's lines so they don't overshadow the markers.

You change the formatting of your data markers and lines using the controls in the Format Data Series dialog. This page's controls allow you to select the chart's marker style, color, size, and other attributes. Similar controls for your chart's lines appear on the Line Color and Line Style pages of the dialog. Using those controls, you could create the chart shown in Figure 6-7.

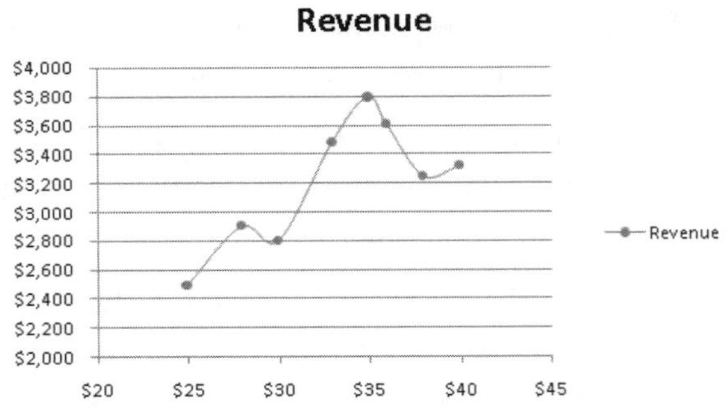

To create the chart in Figure 6-7, you will display the Format

MEMO

The Marker Line Color and Marker Line Style pages of the dialog affect each marker's borders, not the shape or interior color of the marker. If you want your individual data points to stand out, give them a border color that stands out from the marker color and the plot area fill color or pattern.

Figure 6-7   A scatter chart with modified markers and lines

92

Data Series dialog, change the chart's marker style and size, and change the characteristics of the line connecting the markers.

1. Click the chart, and then click Chart Tools | Format to display the Format contextual tab. In the Current Selection group, click the Chart Elements list box's down arrow, and click Series "Revenue." In the same ribbon group, click Format Selection to display the Format Data Series dialog.

2. Click the Marker Options category header to display the dialog page of the same name. Select the Built-in option, click the Type control's down arrow, and click the marker that looks like the sun (it's third from the bottom). Change the value in the Size spin control to 4.

3. Click the Line Style category header to display that dialog page. Edit the value in the Width spin control so that reads 1.25 pt, and then clear the Smoothed Line check box at the bottom of the dialog page. Click Close to dismiss the dialog.

Trend Lines and Scatter Charts

Scatter charts display the results obtained by graphing two sets of values, such as unit price and total sales revenue for a product. When you add a trend line to a chart, Excel uses the values displayed on the horizontal and vertical axes to predict how the value on the vertical axis would be expected to change as the value on the horizontal axis changes.

Excel calculates the trend line using *linear regression* techniques. These calculations aren't simple, but Excel does them for you. In addition to drawing the trend line, Excel can display the trend line's *r-squared* value, which is a measure of how well the trend line fits the data. This calculation is also quite complicated, but you can interpret the results with the knowledge that the closer the r-squared value is to 1.0, the better the trend line fits the data.

Figure 6-8 shows an example of a chart with a trend line already added.

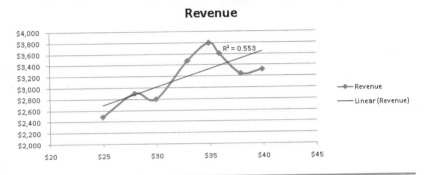

Figure 6-8   A trend line indicates how the values on the horizontal and vertical axes relate.

94

MEMO

The r-squared value for this calculation, 0.553, is low enough to indicate that the equation used to draw the trend line doesn't fit the data very well. That conclusion makes sense for product pricing data, where increasing prices beyond a certain point results in declining sales revenue (plotted on the vertical axis) as the higher prices (plotted on the horizontal axis) discourage more buyers.

To create the chart in Figure 6-8, you will add a trend line to a scatter chart and display the trend line's r-squared value.

1. Open the Excel 2007 file Chap06Trendline.xlsx. The DataSeries worksheet contains a table and scatter chart summarizing sales revenue for a product that was test-marketed at a variety of price points.

2. Click the chart, and then click Chart Tools | Layout | Trendline | More Trendline Options to display the Format Trendline dialog.

3. At the bottom of the Trendline Options page of the dialog, select the Display R-Squared Value on Chart check box, and click Close to dismiss the dialog.

Creating and Formatting a Stock Chart

Excel 2007 provides a powerful set of tools you can use to analyze financial data. Many users track their company's budgets, project expenditures, and overall performance using a combination of worksheet data, formulas, and charts. Financial analysts who track companies' value to their shareholders use one specific tool, the stock chart, to summarize a company's share value and how that value changes over time.

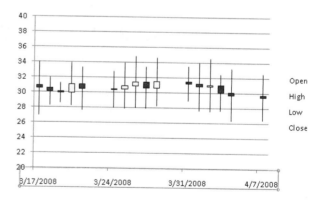

In this chapter, you'll learn how to read, create, and format stock charts, like the one shown in Figure 7-1.

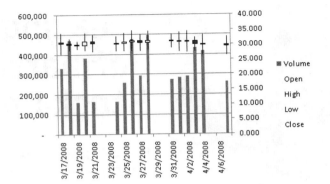

Figure 7-1 A stock chart that summarizes a stock's price and trading volume over a series of days

What Is a Stock Chart?

A stock chart summarizes data relating to a stock's price fluctuations during one or more trading days. The sample chart shown in Figure 7-1 displays the opening, high, low, and closing values of a fictitious company's stock price, plus the number of shares traded on each of those days.

Available Stock Chart Types

Excel 2007 allows you to create four types of stock charts:

- *High-Low-Close* charts, which summarize the highest, lowest, and closing values of a stock for a series of trading days. This stock chart subtype requires three data series, plus a series of stock labels or dates from which the values were collected.

- *Open-High-Low-Close* charts, which summarize the opening, highest, lowest, and closing values of a stock for a series of trading days. This stock chart subtype requires four data series, plus a series of stock labels or dates for which the values were collected.

- *Volume-High-Low-Close* charts, which summarize the number of shares traded, plus the highest, lowest, and closing stock values for

MEMO

Don't confuse a bar stock chart with a regular bar chart. A bar stock chart summarizes stock data by displaying the high, low, and closing values, while a regular bar chart (like a column chart) summarizes data by category.

a series of trading days. This stock chart subtype requires three data series, plus a series of stock labels or dates from which the values were collected.

- *Volume-Open-High-Low-Close* charts, which summarize the number of shares traded, plus the opening, highest, lowest, and closing stock values for a series of trading days. This stock chart subtype requires five data series, plus a series of stock labels or dates from which the values were collected.

Which type of chart you create depends on the data you collected.

Reading a Stock Chart

Once you're familiar with how stock charts represent data, a quick glance reveals important financial information. The first thing you need to know is that stock charts come in two basic varieties: *bar* charts and *candlestick* charts. A bar stock chart appears in Figure 7-2.

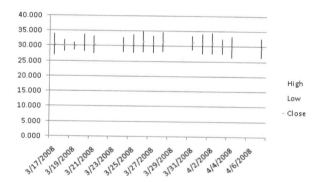

Figure 7-2   This bar stock chart displays high, low, and closing values only.

The stock chart shown in Figure 7-2 summarizes a stock's high, low, and closing values for a series of days. The top of the vertical line indicates the highest value in intraday trading, the bottom of the line indicates the lowest value of that day, and the horizontal bar indicates the closing value. A Volume-High-Low-Close stock chart, such as in Figure 7-1, summarizes stock values using a vertical bar, but in addition, summarizes the number of shares traded each day in a column chart displayed behind the bars in the body of the chart.

MEMO

When you create a Volume-High-Low-Close stock chart, Excel 2007 indicates the magnitude of the share volume using values displayed on the chart's left vertical axis. The chart indicates the relative value of the stock prices using the right vertical axis.

Open-High-Low-Close stock charts, such as the chart shown in Figure 7-3, and Volume-Open-High-Low-Close stock charts display the difference between the opening and closing daily values using a rectangle that has its top and bottom edges at the high and low daily values, respectively.

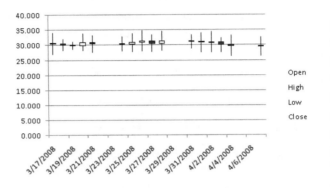

Figure 7-3   This stock chart highlights the difference between opening and closing values.

Because the daily opening or closing value is usually less than the highest value, a vertical line that looks like a candle's wick often extends from the top of the rectangle. This feature led the chart's creators to refer to the charts as *candlestick* charts.

How do you tell the difference between a day where the stock price went up and one where it went down? By the color of the rectangle. Winning days are represented using a white rectangle, while losing days display a black rectangle. You can change those colors, but you might confuse someone who is used to reading charts using the traditional black-and-white color scheme.

Formatting Your Data for a Stock Chart

When you create a chart in Excel 2007, you must make sure your data is arranged so that it makes sense in the chart. Pie charts require a set of categories with matching data; line charts require a series of measurements and a time series; column and bar charts need data reflecting categories and related measures; and so on.

For most types of charts, you can rearrange the data in a chart by clicking Chart Tools | Design | Select Data to display the Select Data Source dialog. From within that dialog you can change the data series and the position of the data displayed in your chart. This technique comes in handy if Excel displays your data incorrectly, such as by misinterpreting a series of years, which should appear on the horizontal axis, as values to be plotted on the vertical axis along with sales or other data.

Stock charts differ from other Excel 2007 chart types in that they require you to have the source table or list formatted exactly as expected. Those expectations are

- The table or data list must contain exactly the data required for the stock chart subtype, with no extraneous columns

- The table columns must be in exactly the right order

- The table columns must contain the right types of data

MEMO

You can name the table columns anything you want—you don't have to give the columns names reflecting each column's role in the chart (open, close, high, low, etc.). That said, it does make sense to give each column the same name as that column's role in the chart. Why? Because then you can verify that the columns contain the expected data and are in the proper order.

As an example, consider a table reflecting a stock's open, high, low, and closing values, plus the dates for which the values were measured. If you were to try and create a High-Low-Close stock chart, Excel would display a message box indicating that the data isn't laid out appropriately for the stock chart subtype you wanted to create.

When you create the data set you want to summarize in a stock chart, Excel verifies that the data source (usually a table) contains the correct number of rows and that those rows contain data of the expected type. In the case of a High-Low-Close stock chart, the chart engine would expect to find a date or stock symbol in the first column and numbers in the remaining three columns.

While the Excel chart engine verifies that the data in each table column is of the proper type, there's no way for the program to determine if the column actually contains the proper data for the chart elements. If you create a table where the columns are in the wrong order, you could end up with nonsensical charts, where the closing value is less than the recorded low for the day.

D3	▾		f_x	33.999		
	A	B	C	D	E	F	G
1							
2		Day	Open	High	Low	Close	
3		3/17/2008	30.875	33.999	27.013	30.506	
4		3/18/2008	30.506	31.958	28.282	30.120	
5		3/19/2008	30.120	31.224	28.672	29.948	
6		3/20/2008	29.948	33.936	28.242	31.089	
7		3/21/2008	31.089	33.328	27.669	30.499	
8		3/24/2008	30.499	32.830	28.014	30.422	
9		3/25/2008	30.422	33.940	27.903	30.921	
10		3/26/2008	30.921	34.815	28.042	31.429	
11		3/27/2008	31.429	33.454	27.891	30.672	
12		3/28/2008	30.672	34.605	28.311	31.458	
13		3/31/2008	31.458	33.503	28.943	31.223	
14		4/1/2008	31.223	34.066	27.708	30.887	
15		4/2/2008	30.887	34.563	27.588	31.076	
16		4/3/2008	31.076	32.477	27.706	30.091	
17		4/4/2008	30.091	33.201	26.396	29.799	
18		4/7/2008	29.799	32.571	26.418	29.494	
19							
20							

Figure 7-4   A properly formatted Excel table

Excel tables and data lists with column headers that reflect the expected values for your chart, such as the table shown in Figure 7-4, make your data more readable and help ensure that your charts turn out well.

To create the table shown in Figure 7-4, you will delete a table column, insert a blank column into the table, change the new column's header, and paste existing data into the column's cells.

1. Open the Excel 2007 file Chap07CreateTable.xlsx. The first page of data contains a table summarizing the stock performance of a fictitious company, plus data to be included in the table in a column to the table's right.

2. Right-click the table cell that contains the Volume column header (cell C2), point to Delete, and then click Table Columns to remove the Volume column from the table.

3. Right-click the cell that contains the Low column header (cell D2), point to Insert, and then click Table Columns to the left. Edit the value in the new column's header cell, which appears in cell D2 (the Low and Close columns were pushed one column to the right) so that it reads High.

4. Select the cell range H3:H18, click Home | Cut, click cell D3, and then click Home | Paste.

Pasting the data into the new table column completes the data set you need to create a stock chart.

MEMO

If you store your data in a regular cell range instead of an Excel 2007 table, you can create room for any new data by adding a column to your worksheet. To do that, right-click the worksheet column header to the left of where you want the new row to appear. In the pop-up menu that appears, click Insert to add the new column.

100

Creating the Chart from Data

Once you have arranged your data into a table or list, you can summarize that data using a stock chart. To create a stock chart, you select any cell in your table, click Insert Other Charts, and then click the desired stock chart subtype from the gallery that appears. You could, for example, create a chart such as the one that appears in Figure 7-5.

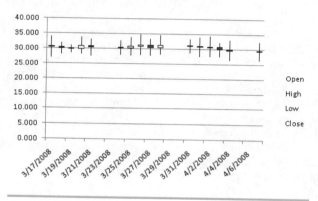

Figure 7-5   A stock chart created from table data

To create the stock chart that appears in Figure 7-5, you will select a cell in the source table and select the desired chart type from the ribbon.

1. Open the Excel 2007 file Chap07MakeChart.xlsx. The first page of data contains a table summarizing the stock performance of a fictitious company.

2. Select any cell in the table, and then click Insert | Other Charts. In the gallery that appears, click the Open-High-Low-Close chart subtype.

After you click the desired chart subtype, Excel verifies that the data is in the expected format and creates the chart.

WHAT YOU SHOULDN'T CHART ON A STOCK CHART

Every chart type and subtype is ideally suited for specific types of data collections. Column and bar charts summarize data by category; line charts summarize data as the values change over time; and pie charts reflect how the values in a data series contribute to the series' total value.

Stock charts summarize stock data quite well. In fact, that's pretty much all they're good for. It can be tempting to summarize other data sets in a stock chart, but the results are usually meaningless or, worse, misleading.

As an example, consider daily temperature data. If you measure a day's high temperature, low temperature, and temperature at midnight (the equivalent of a closing value), you could produce a graph like the one in Figure 7-6.

The graph looks reasonable, but it's not the best way to display the temperature data in the example.

One concern is that the chart's layout implies that the highest temperature occurs during the middle of the day and the lowest occurs at night. Even though those assumptions are often true, changing weather patterns can lead to nighttime temperatures that are higher than the temperature at noon.

In the case of weather data, it's far better to create a line chart that lets you compare high and low values for the day or to compare temperatures for the same time of day across a number of days. A line chart summarizing a set of high and low daily temperatures appears in Figure 7-7.

The conclusion to draw from this analysis is that stock charts are best used to summarize stock price variations and nothing else. If your data varies over time, consider creating a line chart from your data.

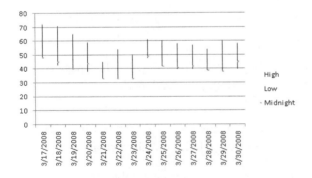

Figure 7-6 This stock chart summarizes temperature data and produces nonsense.

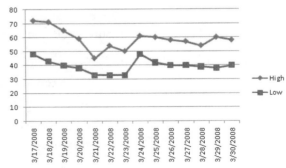

Figure 7-7 A line chart correctly summarizing temperature data

Formatting Your Chart by Hand

You can use the chart styles and layouts presented to change the overall look and feel of your stock chart. If one of the existing chart styles closely approximates the color scheme you want to apply to your chart, you can select the chart, click Chart Tools | Design, and then click one of the styles or layouts that appears in the Chart Layouts and Chart Styles groups' galleries.

If your company has a corporate style guide or color scheme, it's likely that the built-in styles won't reflect your company's standards. If that's the case, you can format any chart element by hand. As with every other chart type, you can select a chart element to format by selecting the chart and then clicking Chart Tools | Format and then, in the Current Selection group, clicking the Chart Elements box's down arrow and selecting the desired element. Clicking the Format Selection button in the same ribbon group displays a dialog with the available formatting options for that element.

In this section, you'll learn how to format the chart's axes, plot area, and data series.

103

Format the Horizontal and Vertical Axes

When you create a chart, Excel formats the chart's horizontal and vertical axes based on the values and formatting present in the source data. For example, if your data source contained stock prices ranging from 0 to 40 and that had three digits to the right of the decimal point, Excel would produce a chart like the one shown in Figure 7-8.

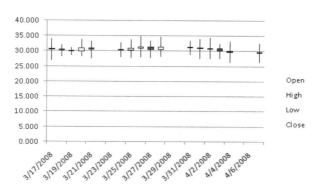

The chart shown in Figure 7-8 displays your data properly, but the relatively

Figure 7-8 Extraneous decimal digits make the vertical axis hard to read.

narrow value range means that the stock chart's markers are squashed into the top of the chart. In addition, the three digits to the right of the decimal point on the vertical axis can make those values harder to read. You can improve your chart's legibility by removing the digits to the right of the decimal point and by limiting the values shown on the axis, increasing the size of the indicators in the body of the chart. The results of such a change appear in Figure 7-9.

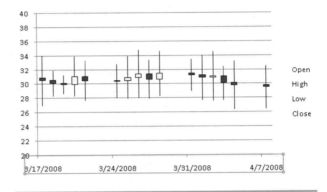

Figure 7-9   A more appropriately formatted vertical axis

MEMO

Because the text on the chart's horizontal axis has a horizontal orientation (with an added tilt) when Excel creates the chart, selecting Horizontal from the Text Direction box won't actually change the text's appearance. That's why you had to change the text's alignment to something other than Horizontal and then change it back to Horizontal to get the desired result.

To create the chart you see in Figure 7-9, you will change the vertical axis so that it is numbered from 20 to 40, format the numbers on the vertical axis so the chart displays them as whole numbers (numbers without digits to the right of the decimal point), and change the alignment of text displayed on the horizontal axis.

1. Open the Excel 2007 file Chap07FormatAxis.xlsx. The first page of data contains a table and a chart summarizing the stock performance of a fictitious company.

2. Right-click any number on the chart's vertical axis, and click Format Axis. Then, if necessary, in the Format Axis dialog's category list, click Axis Options.

3. Next to the Minimum label at the top of the Axis Options page of the dialog, select the Fixed option, and type **20** into the box to the right of the button. Next to the Maximum label, select the Fixed option, and type **40** into the box to the right.

4. In the Format Axis dialog's category list, click Number. Then, in the Decimal Places box, type **0**. Click the Close button to dismiss the Format Axis dialog.

5. Right-click any date on the horizontal axis, and then click Format Axis. In the Format Axis dialog's category list, click Alignment.

6. Click the down arrow in the Text Direction box, and then click Rotate All Text 270°. To change the orientation again, click the Text Direction box's down arrow, and click Horizontal. Click the Close button to close the Format Axis dialog.

The chart's vertical axis now reflects the narrow range of prices within which the stock has traded, and the dates on the horizontal axis appear in horizontal text.

Format a Stock Chart's Data Series

When you create a column chart or a line chart, each data indicator reflects values that are part of a single set of values. For example, a line chart might show a city's high temperatures for every day in May. If you format the data series, you can change the indicators' colors or, in the case of a column chart, change the formatting of the columns.

Stock charts combine several data series into a single display. Those series always include the high, low, and closing stock prices, plus the trading volume and opening values, if you choose to include that data. Because stock charts summarize several data series, you need to format the indicators separately. Those indicators are

- The *High-Low Lines*, which indicate the highest and lowest values from a day's trading

- The *Up Bars,* which are the rectangles displayed when the closing value is higher than the opening value (i.e., the stock increased in price)

- The *Down Bars,* which are the rectangles displayed when the closing value is higher than the opening value (i.e., the stock decreased in price during the day)

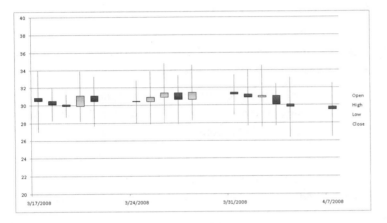

You can format any of these chart elements by clicking one of the elements in the body of the chart, but it might be easier to select the element from the Chart Elements list box on the Chart Tools Format tab. One result of these formatting operations appears in Figure 7-10.

To create the chart you see in Figure 7-10, you will format the chart's data series by changing the color and style of the High-Low Lines and changing the fill colors and effects applied to the Up Bars and the Down Bars.

Figure 7-10 Chart elements formatted to conform to a blue-based color scheme

1. Open the Excel 2007 file Chap07FormatSeries.xlsx. The first page of data contains a table and chart summarizing the stock performance of a fictitious company.

2. If necessary, select the chart, and click Chart Tools | Format to display the Format contextual tab on the ribbon. In the Current Selection group, click the down arrow in the Chart Elements list box at the top of the group, and then click High-Low Lines 1.

3. In the Shape Style group on the ribbon, click the Shape Outline button's down arrow, and click the Blue, Accent 1 color square on the top row of the palette that appears.

4. In the Current Selection group on the ribbon, click the Chart Elements list box's down arrow, and then click Down-Bars 1 to select the bars summarizing the opening and closing values on days when the stock's price declined.

5. In the Shape Styles group on the ribbon, click the Shape Fill button's down arrow, and then click the Blue, Accent 1, Darker 25% color square. To change the shapes' fill pattern, click the Shape Fill button's down arrow again, point to Gradient, and then, in the Dark Variations section of the palette that appears, click the Linear Up pattern.

6. In the Current Selection group on the ribbon, click the Chart Elements list box's down arrow, and then click Up-Bars 1 to select the bars summarizing the opening and closing values on days when the stock's price increased.

7. In the Shape Styles group on the ribbon, click the Shape Fill button's down arrow, point to Gradient, and then, in the Light Variations section of the palette that appears, click the Linear Down pattern.

The formatting you applied to the chart series makes the chart a bit more visually appealing than the standard chart, but without compromising the clarity inherent in black-and-white lines and boxes.

Format a Stock Chart's Plot Area

One way to think of a chart is as an image that has three parts: a frame, a background, and a foreground. The axes are the frame, providing both a visual boundary and context for the chart's contents. Similarly, the data series are the foreground image, relaying the chart's most important details. The chart's plot area serves as the background. When you format a chart's plot area, you should ensure that your changes help the plot area enhance the data rather than hinder it. One example of a reasonably formatted plot area appears in Figure 7-11.

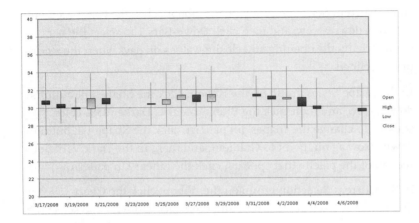

Figure 7-11   Change the plot area's formatting to enhance your data's presentation.

To create the chart you see in Figure 7-11, you will format the plot area by adding a background color and by changing the plot area's border color and line style.

1.   Open the Excel 2007 file Chap07FormatPlotArea .xlsx. The first page of data contains a table and chart summarizing the stock performance of a fictitious company.

2.   If necessary, select the chart, and click Chart Tools | Format to display the Format contextual tab on the ribbon. In the Current Selection group, click the down arrow in the Chart Elements list box at the top of the group, and then click Plot Area.

3.   In the Shape Styles group on the ribbon, click the Shape Fill button's down arrow, and then, in the color palette that appears, click the White, Background 1, Darker 5% color square.

4.   In the Shape Styles group on the ribbon, click the Shape Outline button's down arrow, and then, in the Standard Colors section of the palette that appears, click the Blue square.

5.   Click the Shape Outline button's down arrow again, point to Weight, and then click 1½ point.

The chart's plot area formatting adds sharper definition to the edges of the area, framing your data more effectively, and provides a softer background than the original stark white color.

Creating and Formatting a Surface Chart

Surface charts are unique in that they don't take the traditional two-dimensional approach to display data on a "flat" surface. A little like doughnut charts, discussed in Chapter 9, which *may* compare two data series, a surface chart, *by definition*, compares two data series. What makes a surface chart different from other charts is that instead of having only an x (horizontal) and y (vertical) axis, a surface chart adds a z (depth) axis.

A surface chart may seem to display data in 3-D, but it does not. What a surface chart does, in fact, is connect the three data points together, creating what looks like a topographic map. For a surface chart to have meaning, though, there must be a specific relationship among the three data points: Two of the data points act together and manifest in the third. The third data point doesn't need to be an addition, subtraction, multiplication, or division of the other two. The example in this chapter, for instance, takes two axes of objective data about the workplace (percent utilized and number of people on a team) and creates a z axis of employee job satisfaction.

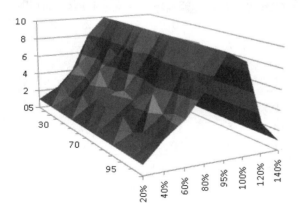

- 8-10
- 6-8
- 4-6
- 2-4
- 0-2

MEMO

An important distinction between surface charts and other charts is that in a surface chart, the different colors in the chart area represent data ranges, rather than data series. Think of it like a topographic map, which shows different elevation ranges as different colors. This type of continuum allows the viewer to understand the relative differences in values easily, without needing to interpret every data point.

A Surface Chart Is Different from an Area Chart

As you saw in an earlier chapter, an area chart is a line chart with the area under the line filled in. At first glance, this may seem to be the same thing as a surface chart. Keep in mind, though, that an area chart only uses the x and y axes to plot a point on the graph. A surface chart takes three points and draws the graph by connecting them. An area chart suggests two things: the magnitude of the combination of two variables (such as more time resulting in more cost), while a surface chart would take the time and cost variables, and include a third data point, such as how time and cost relate to annual salary.

Using Data to Create a Surface Chart

In this chapter, imagine you are a project manager charged with understanding how the number of members making up a team and their percent utilized contribute to their job satisfaction.

Go to the file Chap8Table.xlsx and use the Worker Satisfaction worksheet data to create the charts as described in the book. The data is included in Table 8-1 if you want to input it yourself.

	20%	40%	60%	80%	95%	100%	120%	140%
5	1	2	4	8	10	9	2	1
10	1	3	5	7	10	8	3	1
20	1	2	4	7	10	8	2	1
25	1	2	4.5	7.5	10	8.5	2	1
30	1	3	5.5	7	10	9	3	1
40	1	2	4	8	10	9	2	1
50	1	3.5	4	8.5	10	8	3.5	1

Table 8-1   Team Size (Vertical), Percent Utilized (Horizontal) Lead to Job Satisfaction

MEMO

"Percent utilized" refers to how much of a normal 40-hour workweek the employees are actually working. The example is hypothetical, so I've included ranges from 20 percent to 140 percent. If the percent utilized is below 100 percent, the workers are idle but are still paid for their full workweek. If the percent utilized is over 100 percent, the workers are working their normal workweek plus the extra time (and are paid for it).

	20%	40%	60%	80%	95%	100%	120%	140%
60	1	3	4.5	7	10	8.5	3	1
70	1	2.5	4	7.5	10	9	2.5	1
75	1	3	5	8	10	9.5	3	1
80	1	2	5.5	8	10	8.5	2	1
90	1	2.5	4	8	10	8.5	2.5	1
95	1	2.5	4.5	7.5	10	9	2.5	1
100	1	3	4.5	7	10	9	3	1

Table 8-1   Team Size (Vertical), Percent Utilized (Horizontal) Lead to Job Satisfaction (*cont.*)

Let's go ahead and create a surface chart using this data set.

1. Open the Excel 2007 file Chap8Table.xlsx. The first page contains the Worker Satisfaction data. Alternatively, open a new Excel 2007 file, and input the data from the table (including Column A and Row 1).

2. Click Insert | Chart | Other Charts | Surface to create your chart. The result you get when you click the leftmost chart option is shown in Figure 8-1.

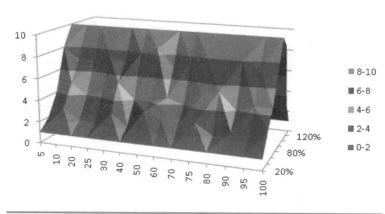

Figure 8-1   Standard formatted surface chart

111

As you can see, the chart is relatively smooth, as there are several data points contributing to it. You can also see on the right side of the chart that there is a "downhill" side to it. It's not easy to see in the default output, so you may want to rotate the chart so you can see it better. To do so:

1. Right-click the chart area, and select 3-D Rotation.

2. In the Format Chart Area dialog that appears, you will have the option to adjust the angles for the x and y axes. Change the axes' angles until you are satisfied with the chart's appearance. Figure 8-2 shows the chart from Figure 8-1 put into a 3-D style with the x axis rotated to 60 percent.

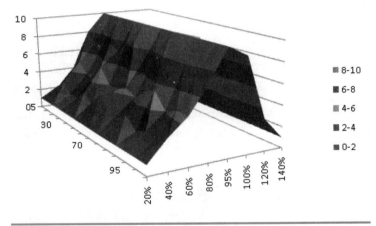

Figure 8-2   Figure 8-1 rotated and put into 3-D

There Are Four Types of Surface Charts

When you go to Insert | Chart | Other Charts | Surface, you will see four different types of surface charts. They are

- **3-D Surface Chart**   This shows value trends across two numeric data series. Figures 8-1 and 8-2 are 3-D surface charts.

■ **Wireframe 3-D Surface Chart** This shows data in a continuous curve, and Microsoft suggests that this chart type be used when the data is both numeric and "curves behind itself." Figure 8-3 is an example of a wireframe 3-D surface chart.

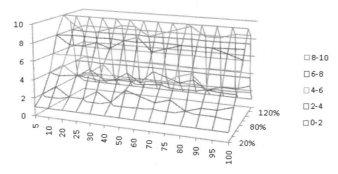

Figure 8-3 Wireframe 3-D surface chart

■ **Contour 3-D Surface Chart** This is a 3-D surface chart as seen from looking down at it and directly above its center. The line colors give a clear representation of the data ranges from both sides of the chart's "hill." Figure 8-4 is an example of a contour 3-D surface chart.

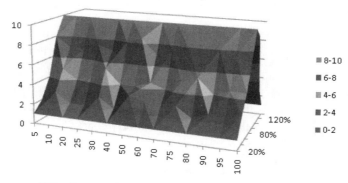

Figure 8-4 Contour 3-D surface chart

■ **Wireframe Contour Chart** This is a contour 3-D surface chart without the color bands filled in. Even Excel 2007 suggests using a regular contour 3-D surface chart rather than this one, so if no other chart type gives you the view you want, try this as a last resort.

Formatting Your Chart by Hand

The charts we've made so far used the default style. To best communicate your intended message, though, you might want to experiment with different chart formats in addition to rotating the axes, such as style, plot area, and data series.

Changing Your Chart's Style

To make a chart more visually appealing, you can apply one of the many available styles to it, which is easy to do in Excel 2007. If you click the chart you've created, the Design | Chart Styles tab will become available. Click around until you find the one you like best. If you don't like the default color bands in the chart, you may want to go back and see if a different style works better than the one you chose previously.

Formatting Your Chart's Plot Area

If you want to format the plot area for your chart, you have the same options available here as you do for the other charts. If you right-click the chart, you will have the option to format the chart area with the following tabs:

- **Fill**   This will change the background color for your chart. If you will be placing the chart into a PowerPoint presentation or Word document, you will likely be able to keep the default white background. Do note, though, that you are able to use a picture as the default fill. If you want to, you can insert your company logo into the background of every chart you do (well, the ones that belong to you, anyway).

- **Border Color**   Each chart you create will have a thin black line around its border. If you are going to be pasting the chart into a presentation or document, you may not want to have that. To get rid of it, simply select the No Line option.

- **Border Styles**   If you want your chart to have a border but don't like the default, you can change the border's thickness and style, as well as other visual effects.

- **Shadow**   If you want to add a little depth to the chart's perspective, you can give it a shadow by selecting where on the chart's border you want it to appear and how light/dark you want it.

- **3-D Format**   Another way to add depth to the chart is to give its border a 3-D effect, such as beveling.

- **3-D Rotation**   As discussed earlier in this chapter, 3-D rotation is an effective way to show the reader your surface chart in a way that gives them the optimal visual perspective.

Changing Sizes

The next thing you can do to make the chart better fit your needs is to change its size. To change your chart's size using the control panes at the top of your screen, click the empty space in your chart, and do the following:

1. Click the Format tab.

2. Select the Size pane.

3. Adjust the size by inputting your desired dimensions into the Height and Width boxes.

THE EASY WAY

Grab one of the chart boxes' corners with your mouse to make the box the size you want. This works particularly well if all you need to do is make it look proportional in a PowerPoint presentation or Word document.

Using the Layout Tab

The next step in refining your formatting is to change the legend's presentation.

1. Select the legend by clicking it.

2. Go to Format | Shape Styles pane, and select a format. You can use the up and down arrows to move row by row through the possibilities or the More arrow (located below the down arrow) to see all available formats at the same time.

3. As you move your cursor across the options, the legend will change temporarily to the one you're hovering over, so you will be able to see how it would look without actually selecting the option. Click the one you want to make the actual change.

4. To format the legend's border and interior fill, you can also go to the Format | Shape Styles pane. When you click the arrows, you will be given different options for

   - **Shape Fill** The fill options, such as color, gradient, and picture.

   - **Shape Outline** The border's line weight and form (solid or dashed line, for example).

   - **Shape Effects** For this, you are able to change the border's edge to include glow effects, shadows, beveling, and even 3-D.

5. To change the legend's font, right-click the box. You will then have the ability to change the font like you do in Word. You also have another link to the fill and border changes available here. Selecting Format Legend at the bottom of the drop-down list will also give you a way to make the fill, border, and shape effects changes.

Adding Chart and Axis Titles to Your Chart

If you want to put your chart's title in the plot area, there's a simple way to do so.

1. Select the white area of your chart.

2. Click Layout | Labels | Chart Title.

3. If you select the arrow on the right side of the Chart Title box, you will be given several options as to where the title should go and whether the chart should be resized automatically. If you put in the title and it changes how the chart looks, make the chart bigger by grabbing a corner and dragging it out. Do so until the chart with the title in it is correctly proportioned.

4. Change the title's formatting (font, color, fill, etc.) by right-clicking it.

To label the axes:

1. Go to Layout | Labels | Axis Titles.

2. You will be able to format the primary horizontal, primary vertical, and depth axes, with options to make the titles read in the directions you want (horizontal, vertical, or rotated), as well as the normal formatting options.

You may also want to tailor the chart's message by inserting some text boxes.

1. Go to Insert | Text | Text Box.

2. Place your cursor within the chart area, and drag it at an angle to create a space to type in. Don't worry that it may not be the right size when you create it. That's easily fixed.

3. Type your text and format it using the Home | Font controls.

4. Adjust the text box's size by dragging on the middle of the top or bottom line to make it taller, on the left or right edge to make it wider, or on a corner to make it both taller and wider.

5. Click and hold anywhere else on the text box's outline to move it where you want it.

Adding Shapes to Your Chart

You may want to include arrows to indicate the connections visually so that your audience will know which words refer to which numbers. To do this:

1. Select Insert | Illustrations | Shapes, which will give you a large number of shapes to choose from. If the arrowed line isn't in Recently Used Shapes, it will be in Lines, the next row down. Figure 8-5 shows some of the available shapes.

2. Move your cursor into the chart's plot area, and draw the arrow. Don't worry if it isn't perfect; you can change the format easily.

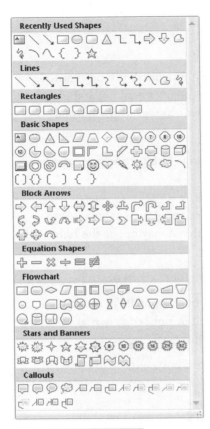

Figure 8-5 Available shapes

3. To change the line's length, select it and use your cursor to grab one of the ends. Drag the end as far as you need to get the line the proper length.

4. To change the line's color and style, right-click the line and select Format Shape. You will then be given several options, much like the ones you've seen before for formatting borders and shading, as shown in Figure 8-6. Most importantly, you will be able to adjust the line's weight and color.

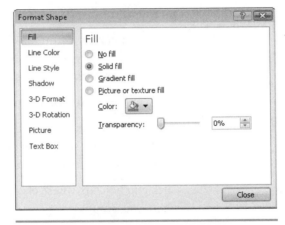

Figure 8-6 Format Shape dialog

Creating a Chart Template

After all your hard work creating your chart, you want to save it as a template so the design can be used over and over again to present a consistent message to your audience! Here's how you do it:

1. Open the chart you want to save as a template.

2. Select Design | Save As Template.

3. Name the template and click Save!

FAQ

FAQ: When should I use a surface chart?

Answer: You should use a surface chart when you have two axes of data that demonstrate a relationship through a third data point.

FAQ: How do I interpret a surface chart?

Answer: Each color band in a surface chart represents a range of the primary vertical (y) axis, much like a topographic map uses different colors to denote ranges of elevation.

Surface charts are a pretty advanced type of chart to use, but if the data you have fit into the model, it is an effective way to relay your message.

Creating and Formatting a Doughnut Chart

The doughnut chart is another way to present data representing parts of a whole. Like pie and bar charts, you can show visually the amount and relative value each piece of the doughnut accounts for. The real power of this type of chart is that you are able to show different series of the same data types side by side for comparison.

Doughnut charts aren't always easy for the human eye to interpret because they are circles, and when two data series are compared, the "slices" representing identical amounts are smaller in the inside rings than in the outside rings. Much like the pie chart, though, the different sections of the doughnut (data series) are different colors, which helps. If you construct an "exploded" doughnut, in which the parts of the chart are separated to more strongly distinguish each slice from the others, you provide an even greater level of clarity to the reader. Figures 9-1 and 9-2 show traditional and exploded doughnut charts. We'll put numbers and words in them later in the chapter.

■ Gold
■ All Other Metals

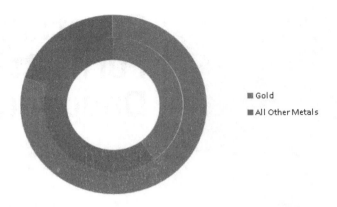

- ■ Gold
- ■ All Other Metals

Figure 9-1   A traditional doughnut chart

MEMO

Because it's more difficult to read doughnut charts than other chart types, it's not generally recommended to use more than five to seven data series in such a chart. One major exception would be to show, for example, how one or two things contribute a disproportionate amount of cost to an organization. You could also use it in the other direction—to show that what should be a large percentage of income is actually much less than desired.

Using Data to Create a Doughnut Chart

In this chapter's examples, imagine you are a project manager responsible for tracking and managing the percent each of five metals contributes to your products' cost. The goal is to keep gold at or below 40 percent; if it goes higher, production changes are expected to bring it back down to that level. Go to the file Chap9Table.xlsx and use the Metal Percent Cost worksheet data to create the charts as described in the book. It's not a lot of data, so I've included it here in Table 9-1 if you want to input it yourself:

	2006	2007
Gold % Cost	40%	50%
Platinum % Cost	20%	20%
Copper % Cost	15%	15%
Iron % Cost	10%	10%
Bronze % Cost	15%	5%

Table 9-1   Metals Cost by Percent

■ Gold
■ All Other Metals

Figure 9-2 An exploded doughnut chart

Here's how to create the charts shown in Figures 9-1 and 9-2.

1. Open the Excel 2007 file Chap9Table.xlsx. The first page contains the Material Percent Cost data. Alternatively, open a new Excel 2007 file and input the data from the table (including the materials and years). For the first two charts, we're only going to use 2006 data.

2. Select the data range you want to include by dragging the appropriate range of cells. For this chart, click cell A1, and hold down the mouse button as you drag your cursor to cell B6. All of the cells in Rows A and B should now be selected.

3. Click Insert | Chart | Other Charts | Doughnut to create your chart. You will notice that you will be able to select both traditional and exploded styles. The chart won't look exactly like the ones in Figures 9-1 and 9-2, because they have had some manual formatting changes made to them. Making those changes will be described later in this chapter.

MEMO

If you want the data to show up as percentages, click the Home tab and click the % symbol on the Number pane.

You should now have one regular and one exploded doughnut chart in your worksheet. Keep them, as you can use them to practice changing your chart's formatting. Let's now create a regular and exploded chart using both 2006 and 2007 data.

1. On the Material Percent Cost page, select cells A1 through C6 by clicking A1 and dragging your cursor to C6. All cells in that range should now be highlighted.

2. Click Insert | Chart | Other Charts | Doughnut to create your chart. The outputs are shown in Figures 9-3 and 9-4.

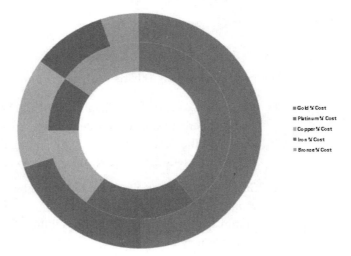

Gold % Cost
Platinum % Cost
Copper % Cost
Iron % Cost
Bronze % Cost

124

Figure 9-3   Traditional doughnut chart using 2006 and 2007 data

By the way: Are these charts not aesthetically pleasing enough for you? Later on, you will see how you can select different chart styles that will make a presentation to your boss look professional-grade.

What Does a Doughnut Chart Show You?

A properly composed doughnut chart makes it clear to a reader the contribution each of a limited number of inputs makes to the "100%" of the total you're addressing. Numbers provide the same information, of course, but as seen throughout this book, there are several ways to present data.

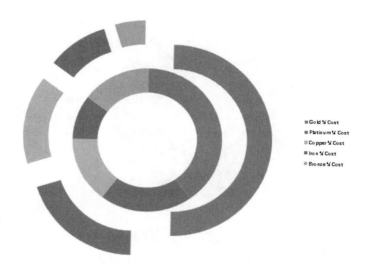

Legend:
- Gold % Cost
- Platinum % Cost
- Copper % Cost
- Iron % Cost
- Bronze % Cost

Figure 9-4 Exploded doughnut chart using 2006 and 2007 data

As long as charts aren't used to distort what the data means, it just makes sense to show it in a way that communicates your message most effectively. If you have a nontechnical audience, they may or may not understand conceptually what the numbers you're presenting mean, but they will likely grasp the significance of the difference between a good number and a bad number, especially for large discrepancies.

For instance, you could use the inner circle to show the ideal number and the outer circle to show an out-of-balance actual number. This is shown in Figure 9-5, using the percent of total metals cost that gold represents versus all other metals. You can re-create this chart using the Gold Optimal Versus Actual sheet in the Chap9Table.xlsx file. Select cells A1 through C3, and create the chart as detailed previously.

There are limitations to the types of data you can show in a doughnut chart. For instance, you can't show negative or zero values because they can't be included as part of the "whole." Line and bar charts are best to show negatives and zeros.

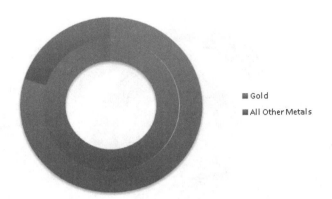

■ Gold
■ All Other Metals

Figure 9-5   Total percent gold cost versus all other metals

Formatting Your Chart by Hand

The charts we've made so far used the default style. They're functional and convey the desired information, but they have some obvious shortcomings. For one, they aren't very pretty. Something else that could be done is to add numbers to the chart, which would help reinforce its message.

To make a chart more visually appealing, you can apply one of many available styles to it, which is easy to do in Excel 2007. If you click the chart you've created, the Design | Chart Styles tab will become available. You can give the chart a 3-D aspect either by paging down to one of the last rows and selecting your preferred style or by selecting the bottom arrow at the right edge of the Chart Styles tab to display all available styles. The result is shown in Figure 9-6.

Changing Sizes

The next thing you can do to make the chart better fit your needs is to change its size and/or the size of the doughnut hole. To change your chart's size using the panes at the top of your screen, click the empty space in your chart, and do the following:

1. Click the Format tab.

2. Select the Size pane.

THE EASY WAY

Grab one of the chart box's corners with your mouse to make the box the size you want. This works particularly well if all you need to do is make it look proportional in a PowerPoint presentation or Word document.

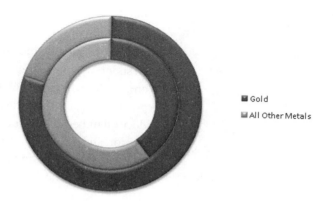

Figure 9-6 Doughnut chart rendered with 3-D effects

3. Adjust the size by inputting your desired dimensions into the Height and Width boxes.

The default setting for the doughnut hole may not be to your liking. To change it:

1. Click your chart.

2. Select Format | Current Selection | Format Selection.

3. You will then see the Doughnut Hole Size slider at the bottom of the box. It can be as small as 10 percent and as large as 90 percent. Adjust it to your liking.

4. You may also want to go back to the Design | Chart Styles tab and experiment to see if a new style looks better after you've changed the size of the doughnut hole.

THE EASY WAY

You can open the same box by right-clicking a data series (one of the doughnut "slices") and selecting Format Data Series.

Using the Rest of the Format Data Series Dialog Capabilities

When you changed the doughnut hole size, you no doubt saw several other opportunities to make the chart more to your liking, which will now be discussed. Figure 9-7 shows the Format Data Series dialog.

127

Figure 9-7   Format Data Series dialog

On the Series Options tab, you are also able to rotate the doughnut slices around the circle for the best visual impact. By moving the Angle of First Slice slider, you can adjust where the slice you want to emphasize will appear on the chart, enabling you to put additional information in the chart, slide, or document beside it if you want. The Doughnut Explosion slider lets you determine how much you want the outer doughnut to be separated from the inner one, if you want to create that effect.

The Fill box gives you several options for changing the doughnut slices themselves, including a gradient, a texture, solid colors, or even a picture from a file. You also have the option of having no fill at all. For example, does your organization use specific colors to represent certain bits of data, your organization, or other organizations? If you do, incorporating them into the chart's color scheme makes sense.

The Border Colors, Border Styles, and Shadows pages allow you to enhance your chart's readability by adding contrast to the edges of selected (or all) slices.

The next step in refining your formatting is to change the legend's presentation. The default rendering is unexciting, to say the least, but Excel 2007 gives you excellent ways to design it according to your preferences.

1. Select the legend by clicking it.

2. Go to Format | Shape Styles pane, and select a format. You can use the up and down arrows to move row by row through the possibilities or the More arrow (located below the down arrow) to see all available formats at the same time.

3. As you move your cursor across the options, the legend will change temporarily to the one you're hovering over, so you will be able to see how it would look without actually selecting the option. Click the one you want to make the actual change.

4. To format the legend's border and interior fill, you can also go to the Format | Shape Styles pane. When you click the arrows, you will be given different options for

   ■ **Shape Fill**   The fill options, such as color, gradient, and picture.

   ■ **Shape Border**   The border's line weight and form (solid or dashed line, for example).

   ■ **Shape Effects**   For this, you are able to change the border's edge to include glow effects, shadows, beveling, and even 3-D.

5. To change the legend's font, right-click the box, producing what you see in Figure 9-8. You will then have the ability to change the font like you do in Word. You also have another link to the fill and border changes available here. Selecting Format Legend at the bottom of the drop-down list will also give you a way to make the fill, border, and shape effects changes.

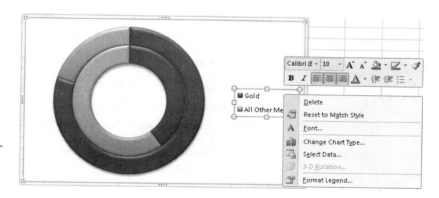

Figure 9-8   Right-clicking the legend and selecting Format Legend

Adding Data Labels
and Text Boxes to Your Chart

Doughnut charts show relative proportions quite well when only using the slices, but the chart's message becomes even more powerful by adding data labels (numbers). Adding the numbers is easy.

1. Right-click one of your data series. You will be given the option to Add Data Labels.

2. Repeat step 1 for each of the data series (rings) in your chart.

3. To change the font color, select each of the data labels, and use the Home | Font pane.

4. If you don't want to have the numbers inside the slices, simply drag the number to where you want it.

After putting numbers in, you may also want to add to the chart's message by inserting some text boxes, especially if a title wasn't generated automatically when you created the chart.

1. Go to Insert | Text | Text Box.

2. Place your cursor within the chart area, and drag it at an angle to create a space to type in. Don't worry that it may not be the right size when you create it. That's easily fixed.

3. Type your text and format it using the Home | Font controls.

4. Adjust the text box's size by dragging on the middle of the top or bottom line to make it taller, on the left or right edge to make it wider, or on a corner to make it both taller and wider.

5. Click and hold anywhere else on the text box's outline to move it where you want it.

Adding Shapes to Your Chart

You may want to include arrows to indicate the connections visually so that your audience will know which words refer to which numbers. To do this:

1. Select Insert | Illustrations | Shapes, which will give you a large number of shapes to choose from. If the arrowed line isn't in Recently Used Shapes, it will be in Lines, the next row down.

2. Move your cursor into the chart's plot area, and draw the arrow. Don't worry if it isn't perfect; you can change the format easily.

3. To change the line's length, select it and use your cursor to grab one of the ends. Drag the end as far as you need to get the line the proper length.

4. To change the line's color and style, right-click the line and select Format Shape. You will then be given several options, much like the ones you've seen before for formatting borders and shading. Most importantly, you will be able to adjust the line's weight and color.

Formatting the Chart's Background

If this chart is going into a PowerPoint presentation or a Word document, you may not need to change the chart's plot area (background). In these cases, the default white background is exactly what you need. If you do want to change the plot area, however, it's easy to do, and Excel 2007 has a lot of good design options.

1. In your open Excel 2007 chart, right-click in the chart's empty space.

2. Select Format Chart Area. The resulting dialog will look familiar from the earlier parts of this chapter. You will have the opportunity to select several different kinds of fill, including Solid, Gradient, Picture, or Texture and Automatic. There will also be an option to adjust the fill's transparency.

3. When you're done, click Close and check out your new background.

Figure 9-9 shows a chart constructed using all the techniques outlined in this chapter.

1. Open the Chap9Table.xlsx Excel 2007 file, and click the Gold Optimal Versus Actual tab.

2. Select cells A1–C3.

3. Choose Insert | Charts | Other Charts | Doughnut.

4. After the chart is created, change its style to the style of your choice (Figure 9-9 uses the default chart colors rendered in 3-D).

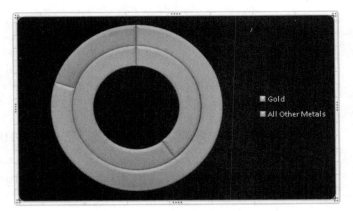

Figure 9-9   Completed doughnut chart

5. Right-click each data series, and select Format Data Series. Use the available options to add borders to your chart to add contrast. In the same dialog, you will be able to rotate the doughnut slices to your liking by using the Angle of First Slice slider.

6. Right-click the legend, and change its appearance and location by selecting Format Location.

7. Right-click each data series, and select Add Data Labels to insert each slice's numeric value. Highlight the number's box, and then go to the Home | Font pane to change the font's color, size, and appearance.

8. Add text boxes to the chart by selecting Insert | Text | Text Box.

9. Add arrows or other shapes by selecting Insert | Illustrations | Shapes.

10. Finally, format the chart's plot area by right-clicking the area and selecting Format Chart Area. Use the available options to change the plot area's appearance to your liking.

Creating a Chart Template

After all your hard work creating your chart, you want to save it as a template so the design can be used over and over again to present a consistent message to your audience! Here's how you do it:

1. Open the chart you want to save as a template.

2. Select Design | Save As Template.

3. Name the template and click Save!

When you need to show some data series side by side and don't have any negative or zero values in your data, the doughnut chart is a great way to do it! The best part is that with Excel 2007, it's easy to make your chart nice to look at by using 3-D formatting.

FAQ

FAQ: When should I use a doughnut chart?

Answer: You should use a doughnut chart when the point you're trying to make is best expressed by comparing multiple data series side by side as proportions.

FAQ: When can't I use a doughnut chart?

Answer: A doughnut chart does not work if you have any negative or zero values.

Creating and Formatting a Bubble Chart

Like a scatter (XY) chart, bubble charts summarize data series where each of the series contains values, not categories. Where scatter (XY) charts plot two data series, bubble charts summarize three series. Like a scatter (XY) chart, both the horizontal and vertical axes contain values that Excel uses to determine where to plot each data point in the body of the chart. Unlike scatter (XY) charts, however, bubble charts change the indicators' size to reflect the relative magnitude of the values in the third data series.

Bubble charts are most useful for plotting financial and scientific data. For example, you could record the temperature and humidity at noon, and measure the rainfall (if any) on that day. In the financial world, you could measure a company's net revenue and profit, and note how much the company's stock gained or lost value on the day the results were announced.

In this chapter you will learn how to create a bubble chart (such as the chart displayed in Figure 10-1), format your charts by hand, and add trend lines to your charts.

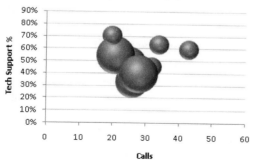

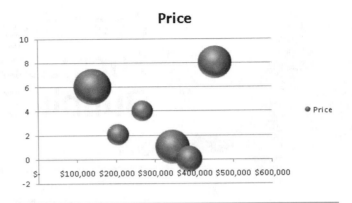

Figure 10-1   A sample bubble chart

Creating the Chart from Data

The easiest way to create a bubble chart is to base it on data stored in a table or list that contains three columns of values. To create a bubble chart from a three-column data set, you click any cell in the table or list, click Insert Other Charts, and click the bubble chart subtype you want to create.

When you create a bubble chart from a three-column data set, Excel 2007 uses the values in the left column as the data source for the horizontal axis, the values in the center column as the data source for the vertical axis, and the values in the right column to determine the size of the bubble. The chart shown in Figure 10-2, for example, indicates the percentage of technical support calls on the horizontal axis, the number of calls per day on the vertical axis, and the number of issues raised per call by varying the size of the bubbles.

Changing the order of the data columns, therefore, affects how Excel charts your data. For example, rearranging the table's data columns so that the left column contained the number of calls per day, the center column contained the number of issues raised per call, and the right column contained the percentage of calls with a technical support component, your chart would look like the one shown in Figure 10-3.

MEMO

Bubbles can obscure other bubbles if they're too close together, so be sure to make your bubble charts as large as possible.

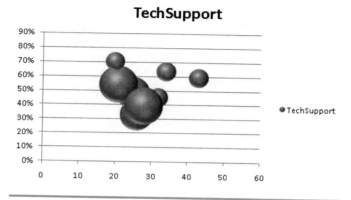

Figure 10-2 Bubble sizes indicate the magnitude of a third data series.

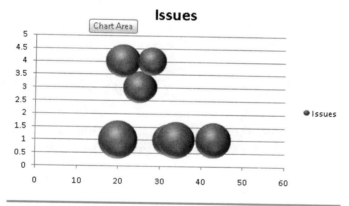

137

Figure 10-3 Changing the order of the data series affects the chart's appearance.

If your data source contains more than three columns of data, you can select the table or data list columns you want to include in the chart, click Insert | Other Charts, and then click the bubble chart subtype you want to create. As with a three-column data source, Excel plots the left column's values on the horizontal axis, the center column's values on the vertical axis, and the right column's values to indicate the bubbles' size.

To create the chart shown in Figure 10-3, you will select a cell in a three-column table and use the controls on the user interface to create the chart. You will then switch worksheets and create a new chart from a four-column table, which requires you to select the columns you want to include in the chart.

1. Open the Excel 2007 file Chap10CreateBubble.xlsx. The Issues worksheet contains a table summarizing customer service calls received by a fictitious company.

2. Click any cell in the table, and then click Insert | Other Charts | Bubble with a 3-D Effect.

3. Click the ExtraData worksheet tab to display the worksheet of the same name. In the table, select the cell range B2:C10, hold down the CTRL key, and select the cell range E2:E10.

4. Release the CTRL key, and click Insert | Other Charts | Bubble with a 3-D Effect.

Formatting Your Chart by Hand

The bubble charts Excel 2007 creates by default don't have a lot of formatting added. These basic charts are fairly easy to read, but they're also a bit plain. If you'd like to dress your charts up a bit, whether to improve their visual impact or to make them conform to your company's graphics standards, you can do so quickly.

Format Plot Area

A bubble chart's plot area contains the data displayed, or plotted, in the body of the chart. When Excel creates the chart, it includes a plot area with a blank, white background and no border. If you want to change the plot area's formatting, you can change the background, or fill, so that it is a solid color, a pattern, or a texture.

Excel creates a texture by repeating an image file enough times to fill the background of your chart. You can select an existing texture or use a picture on your computer, but be sure that the image has no obvious edges and no elements that stand out. Either of these characteristics will draw a viewer's eye to the background and away from the data, which limits your chart's effectiveness.

If you add a texture to your chart's plot area, you might consider adding a border as well. Because good textures don't have identifiable borders, the repeated image can tend to draw the viewer's eye toward the edge of the plot area, away from the body of the chart. Adding a border, such as the one in Figure 10-4, limits that distraction.

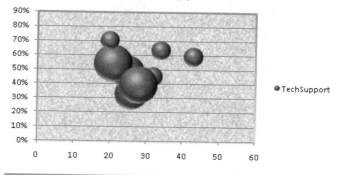

Figure 10-4   Adding a border to the plot area helps focus attention on your data.

To create the chart shown in Figure 10-4, you will format the plot area by adding a newsprint texture fill and a line border with a gradient fill effect.

1. Open the Excel 2007 file Chap10FormatLines.xlsx. The Issues worksheet contains a table and bubble chart summarizing customer service calls received by a fictitious company.

2. Click the chart, and then click Chart Tools | Format to display the Format contextual tab. In the Current Selection group on the ribbon, click the Chart Elements list box's down arrow, and select Plot Area. Click Format Selection to display the Format Plot Area dialog.

Excel 2007 Charts Made Easy

3. In the Fill page of the Format Plot Area dialog, select the Picture or Texture Fill option. Click the Texture button's down arrow, and click the Newsprint texture (it's in the center of the palette that appears).

4. Click the Border Color category, and then select the Gradient Line option. Click the Preset Colors button's down arrow, and click the Daybreak pattern (fourth from the left in the top row.)

5. Click the Border Styles category, and use the Width spin control to set the value to 2 pt. Click Close to dismiss the dialog.

Format Data Series

By default, Excel 2007 draws all bubbles the same color in bubble charts. The data points are all part of the same series, so it makes sense that Excel follows its normal practice of drawing all data points from a series using the same color. This consistency reduces the contrast among the chart's bubbles, which can make it difficult to determine where each bubble begins and ends. If you would like to have Excel draw each bubble with a unique fill color, you can right-click any bubble in the series, click Format Data Series, click the Fill category, and select the Vary Color By Point check box.

If desired, you can change a specific bubble's color. Click any bubble in the chart, and then click the bubble you want to change to select it individually. Right-click the bubble, click Format Data Point, click the Fill category, and use the controls that appear to select a new color for the bubble.

If your data series contains negative values, you can plot them in a bubble chart by right-clicking any bubble, clicking Format Data Series, clicking the Series Options category (if necessary), and then selecting the Show Negative Bubbles check box. When the negative values occur in a column that provides values for the horizontal or vertical axis, Excel 2007 adds negative values to the appropriate axis (or axes). If the negative values occur in the column that determines the size of the chart's bubbles, Excel 2007 displays negative bubbles in white.

THE EASY WAY

If you find that one or more of your bubbles are hidden by other bubbles, change the data series' fill to a lighter color so that the hidden bubbles' outlines show through the ones obscuring them. It's better that you don't use a white fill, though; as you'll see later in this chapter, white bubbles can indicate negative values.

140

Regardless of whether a bubble represents a positive or negative value, the bubble's size reflects the value's distance from zero (its *absolute value*). As shown in Figure 10-5, the values 20% and –20% would generate bubbles of the same size, but Excel displays the positive value using a bubble that's one of the chart's normal colors and displays the negative value's bubble in white.

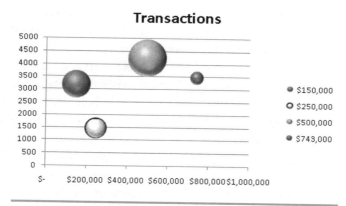

Figure 10-5   How a bubble chart displays positive and negative values with the same absolute value

To create the chart in Figure 10-5, you will set Excel to display each data point using a different color bubble and then have the chart display negative values.

1. Open the Excel 2007 file Chap10BubbleColors.xlsx. The Data worksheet contains a table and bubble chart summarizing revenue, transactions, and change in revenue for a fictitious auto dealership.

2. Click the chart, right-click any bubble, and then click Format Data Series. On the Series Options page of the dialog, select the Show Negative Bubbles check box.

3. Click the Fill category, and then select the Vary Colors By Point check box. Click Close to dismiss the dialog.

MEMO

You can't change the color of bubbles that display negative values. They must be white.

141

Format the Axis

When you create a bubble chart in Excel 2007, the chart doesn't include labels for the values on either the horizontal or vertical axis. This lack of information can make the data hard to interpret, so you should strongly consider adding labels to the axes.

To add a label to the horizontal axis, click the chart and then click Chart Tools | Layout | Axis Titles | Primary Horizontal Axis Title | Title Below Axis. A text box with the words *Axis Title* appears below the horizontal axis. Edit the text in the box to reflect the values displayed on the horizontal axis. To add a label to the vertical axis, click the chart and then click Chart Tools | Layout | Axis Titles | Primary Vertical Axis Title | Rotated Title.

If you create a relatively small bubble chart, you could find that the horizontal gridlines Excel includes to delineate the values on the vertical axis make your chart's body too busy for your liking. If that's the case, you can change the lines' color to make them less obtrusive. To change the horizontal lines' color, right-click any of the gridlines, and click Format Gridlines. In the Format Major Gridlines dialog, select the Solid Line option (note that No Line is not available as an option), click the Color button, and select the desired line color. One such configuration appears in Figure 10-6.

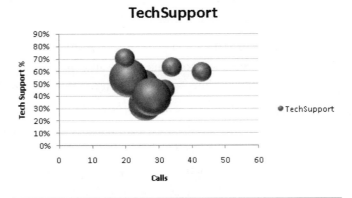

Figure 10-6   Changing gridline colors can reduce visual clutter.

To create the chart in Figure 10-6, you will add labels to the chart's horizontal and vertical axes and then change the horizontal gridlines' color to a light shade of gray.

1. Open the Excel 2007 file Chap10AxesAndLines.xlsx. The Data worksheet contains a table and bubble chart summarizing customer service calls received by a fictitious company.

2. Click the chart, and then click Chart Tools | Layout | Axis Titles | Primary Horizontal Axis Title | Title Below Axis to display the title. Select the text in the text box that appears below the axis, and type **Calls**.

3. Click the chart and then click Chart Tools | Layout | Axis Titles | Primary Vertical Axis Title | Rotated Title. Select the text in the text box that appears to the left of the axis, and type **Tech Support %**.

4. In the Current Selection group on the ribbon, click the Chart Elements list box's down arrow, and then click Vertical (Value) Axis Major Gridlines. Click the Format Selection button to display the Format Major Gridlines dialog.

5. On the Line Color page of the dialog, select the Solid Line option, click the Color button's down arrow, and click the White, Background 1, Darker 15% color square. Click Close to dismiss the dialog.

Trend Lines and Bubble Charts

Like scatter (XY) charts, bubble charts display the results obtained by combining two sets of values (e.g., temperature and humidity), with a third measure (such as rainfall) added to define the size of each bubble. When you add a trend line to a chart, Excel uses the values displayed on the horizontal and vertical axes to predict how the value on the vertical axis would be expected to change as the value on the horizontal axis changes.

Excel makes the calculations using a technique called *linear regression*. The math is fairly complex, but the program does all the work for you. In addition to drawing the trend line, Excel can display the data set's *r-squared* value, which is a measure of how closely the trend line fits the data set. This calculation is also quite complicated, but the general rule is that the closer the r-squared value is to 1.0, the better the trend line fits the data set.

Figure 10-7 shows an example of a chart with a trend line already added.

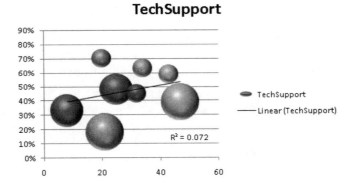

Figure 10-7 A trend line indicates how the values on the horizontal and vertical axes relate.

144

To create the chart in Figure 10-7, you will add a trend line to a bubble chart and display the trend line's r-squared value.

1. Open the Excel 2007 file Chap10Trendline.xlsx. The Data worksheet contains a table and bubble chart summarizing customer service calls received by a fictitious company.

2. Click the chart, and then click Chart Tools | Layout | Trendline | Linear Trendline.

3. In the Current Selection group on the ribbon, click the Chart Elements list box's down arrow, and then click Series "TechSupport" Trendline 1. Click the Format Selection button to display the Format Trendline dialog.

4. At the bottom of the Trendline Options page of the dialog, select the Display R-Squared Value on Chart check box. Click Close to dismiss the dialog. In the chart, drag the r-squared value to a blank area of the chart so that it is visible.

Creating and Formatting a Radar Chart

The radar chart allows you to present data in a way similar to a bar chart, with distinct data categories (such as hours, days, or months). The way radar charts differ, though, is that they are circular in orientation rather than horizontal or vertical, which allows each data category to have its own axis. The term "radar chart" comes from the chart's close resemblance to a radar screen, like the ones found in planes, ships, and submarines. They are also called "spider charts" because they also look like a spider's web.

Radar charts are effective at comparing data values for many different values, such as time periods. An intuitive way to do this is to analyze manufacturing productivity and safety between midnight and noon, which is best shown in a clock-like radar chart display. Clocks are easily understood, and the farther out from the center the data points appear, the greater their value. Figure 11-1 shows a sample radar chart.

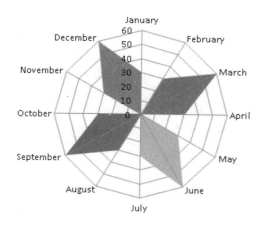

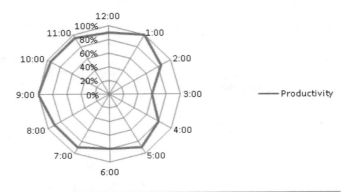

Figure 11-1   A sample radar chart

Using Data to Create a Radar Chart

In this chapter's examples, you are a project manager responsible for monitoring worker productivity and workplace safety at your company's production facility. Company management wants to know how actual productivity matches up against the goal (represented as 100% on the charts) and how actual workplace safety compares to desired levels (also represented as 100%). Your task is to collect the information for each hour between midnight and noon for a month and present it to your superiors. Because the data is to be presented for each hour, a radar chart is a great way to display it.

To create your chart, go to the file Chap11Table.xlsx and use the Productivity and Safety worksheet data as described. If you want to input it yourself, the data is also found in Table 11-1.

Here's how to create the chart shown in Figure 11-1:

1. Open the Excel 2007 file Chap11Table.xlsx. The first page contains the Productivity and Safety data you will be using for this chapter's exercises.

MEMO

One thing that might be confusing about radar charts for someone who's not used to seeing them is that the data values are shown on circles spreading out from the chart's center instead of on either the horizontal or vertical axis, like you see on many other charts.

MEMO

To have the hours formatted as "time," highlight Column A, select Home | Number | Time, and select how you want the data displayed. If you want the data to show up as percentages, click the Home tab, and click the "%" symbol on the Number pane.

	Productivity	Safety
12:00	90%	85%
1:00	100%	60%
2:00	85%	50%
3:00	60%	50%
4:00	80%	75%
5:00	90%	95%
6:00	80%	85%
7:00	90%	100%
8:00	90%	85%
9:00	100%	60%
10:00	95%	90%
11:00	95%	80%

Table 11-1   Productivity and Safety

THE EASY WAY

Grab one of the chart boxes' corners with your mouse, and drag it out until the chart is the size you want. This works particularly well if all you need to do is make it look proportional in a PowerPoint presentation or Word document.

2. Select the data range you want to include by dragging the appropriate range of cells. For this chart, click cell A1 and hold down the left mouse button as you drag your cursor to cell B13. All of the cells in Rows A and B should now be selected.

3. Click Insert | Chart | Other Charts | Radar to create your chart. Figure 11-1 is the option on the far left: an unfilled interior with the values for each circle labeled.

One thing you may notice in your initial output is that the chart isn't very readable because the numbers on the circles are mashed together. You can change the chart's size by selecting the chart and then selecting Chart Tools | Format | Size from the menus on the top of the screen.

Ways to change the chart's formatting to make it fit better into your document or presentation template will be covered later in the chapter.

The Different Types of Radar Charts

There are three varieties of radar charts in Excel 2007: the regular radar chart, the radar chart with markers (where the data points are labeled with a marker), and the filled radar chart (where the output's outline is filled with color). The examples found in the program may be found by opening Excel | Chap11Table.xlsx and selecting all the cells in Columns A and B. Then click Insert | Chart | Other Charts | Radar to see the three different types of radar charts, which are shown in Figure 11-2. Each of the chart types is useful, but not in every situation, as we'll see in the examples that follow.

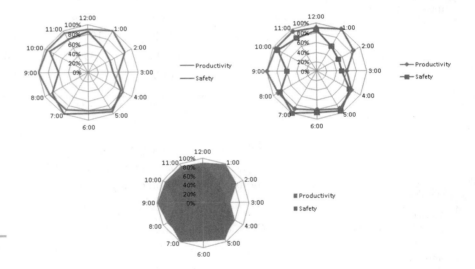

Figure 11-2 The three types of radar charts

What Does a Radar Chart Show You?

As mentioned briefly earlier in the chapter, a radar chart is good at comparing data from one or more data series across several different time periods or, for example, divisions in a company. It is possible, however, to go too far in trying to use a radar chart to make your point.

First, the data you have may not lend itself to a visually appealing radar chart output. As you saw in Figure 11-1, a single data series shown over 12 hours is an ideal situation in which to use a radar chart. For the next example, though, let's see how using both data series looks in a radar chart.

1. Open the Excel 2007 file Chap11Table.xlsx and then select Productivity and Safety.

2. Click cell A1 and drag your cursor down to cell C13.

3. Click Insert | Chart | Other Charts | Radar to create your chart. For this exercise, select the middle chart option, the radar chart with markers. The resulting chart is shown in Figure 11-3.

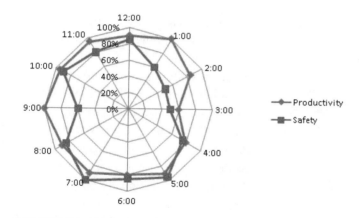

Figure 11-3   Productivity and safety radar chart with markers

As you can see, this chart gives a clear representation of the productivity and safety data collected for each hour. Productivity is pretty close to the goal most of the time, but safety is a major problem from 1:00 until 4:00. As a project manager, you now have some information you need to begin to figure out why this is the case and, more importantly, try to understand what can be done to ensure workers have fewer accidents.

In a lot of cases, all three types of radar charts will not be equally useful in displaying your data. The productivity and safety data is a great example of this, as the filled radar chart doesn't look nearly as good as the regular radar chart and the radar chart with markers. To see this, repeat the steps from the exercise used to create Figure 11-3, but select the filled radar chart option. Because so much of the data overlaps, the intended message (that there is a big drop in safety for a while) is lost. But when would a filled radar chart be the best way to display your data?

A great time to use a filled radar chart is when there is little or no overlap in your data. The example we'll look at is products intended for use during specific seasons. To create your chart:

1. Open the Excel 2007 file Chap11Table.xlsx. The second worksheet contains the seasonal data you will be using for this exercise.

2. Click cell A1 and hold down the left mouse button as you drag your cursor to cell E13. All of the cells in Rows A through E should now be selected.

3. Click Insert | Chart | Other Charts | Radar to create your chart. The filled radar chart is the option on the far right. The chart you create is shown in Figure 11-4.

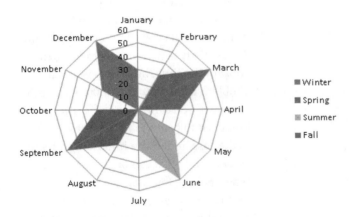

Figure 11-4   Seasonal radar chart

As you can see from the figure, the seasonal data is well suited for a filled radar chart. Sales begin in the first month, peak in the second month, and tail off in the third month of each of the four seasons. Like the 12-hour clock model for the productivity and safety charts, the 12-month calendar layout of Figure 11-4 gives a clear and understandable data display. If you were a manager in charge of making sure enough (but not too much) stock of each seasonal good is available for sale, you would be able to take this information and "count backward" to make sure you have coordinated with your suppliers far enough in advance to have your stock on hand.

Formatting Your Chart by Hand

The charts we've made so far used the default style for each of the three different types of radar charts. To make a chart more visually appealing, you can apply one of the many available styles to it, which is easy to do in Excel 2007. If you click the chart you've created, the Design | Chart Styles tab will become available. You can make the chart you created for Figure 11-4 three-dimensional either by paging down to one of the last rows and selecting your preferred style or by selecting the bottom arrow at the right edge of the Chart Styles tab to display all available styles. The result is shown in Figure 11-5. Go ahead and keep the chart open, as we will be working to change the chart and plot area formatting next.

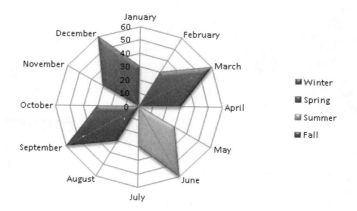

Figure 11-5   Figure 11-4 rendered with 3-D effects

Formatting the Chart and Plot Areas

If this chart is going into a PowerPoint presentation or a Word document, you may not need to change the chart's background. In these cases, the default white background is exactly what you need. If you do want to change the chart and plot areas, however, it's easy to do, and Excel 2007 has a lot of good design options.

1. In your open Excel 2007 chart, right-click in the chart's empty space outside of the data, and select Format Chart Area

151

2. You will have the opportunity to select several different kinds of fill, including Solid, Gradient, Picture or Texture, and Automatic. There will also be an option to adjust the fill's transparency. When you select a color, it will show up on the chart as a preview.

3. When you're done, click Close and check out your new background, as shown in Figure 11-6.

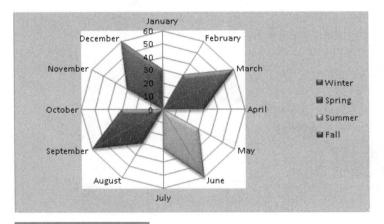

Figure 11-6   Chart area filled with a background

To do the same thing a different way, you could also click the chart and then click Layout | Current Selection | Chart Area (from the drop-down menu) | Format Selection, which will give you the same choices as the previous steps.

Formatting Data Series

If you have a chart with several data series that run together visually, you may want to have a way of setting them apart, which can be accomplished by changing the format of the line in a radar chart or radar chart with markers. For this exercise, we'll use the Productivity and Safety worksheet.

1. Open the Excel 2007 file Chap11Table.xlsx, and select the Productivity and Safety worksheet.

2. Click cell A1 and drag your cursor down to cell C13.

3. Click Insert | Chart | Other Charts | Radar to create your chart. Select the middle chart option, the radar chart with markers.

Now, right-click one of the lines in chart showing either productivity or safety information. Select Format Data Series. In the dialog that appears, select Line Style, and then select Dash Type. Choose one of the dashed lines, then click Close, and you will see your newly formatted data series. You can even change the line color to conform to a standard presentation format (such as if you always use orange to display fall-related numbers).

Keep the chart open, as we will work on formatting the axes and gridlines next.

Formatting Axes and Gridlines

Finally, you may want to change the format of the axes (the lines radiating out of the chart's center) or the gridlines (the lines circling around the center). To do this:

1. Right-click one of the axes, which will display the Format Axis, Format Major Gridlines, or Add Minor Gridlines options. Minor gridlines are lines between the major gridlines that give your data a more precise value to the viewer's eye. If the chart area is small, however, it will likely make the chart more difficult to read.

2. Select Format Axis. You will have the usual options for changing line styles. If, for instance, you want to make the axis stand out more than the gridlines, you can select Line Style | Width to change the line's size. You can also select Line Color to make the axis a color other than gray. If you select Fill from the Format Axis dialog, you can change the color of the boxes the axis values show up in.

3. Now, right-click a gridline. The second option from the bottom will be Format Gridlines. You will have the same options as before. Let's say you want to de-emphasize your chart's gridlines. Select Line Style | Width, and make the line narrower. You could also select Line Style | Dash and make the line a faint dash. That way, the line is still visible, but the axis gets all the attention from the viewer.

Radar charts aren't as common as bar, pie, and line charts, but they do a great job of displaying time-series data. If you need to make a point showing differences or similarities across several points, a radar chart will show how the data conforms or doesn't conform to expectations.

FAQ

FAQ: How would I show the data does or doesn't conform to expectations?

Answer: A great way to do this is to create a data series using the expected results. When you put your actual results in the same chart, the viewer should have a clear picture of how the actual data conforms or doesn't conform to expectations.

FAQ: When should I not use a radar chart?

Answer: If you have only a few data points, such as results twice a year, a radar chart isn't the best way to show the data. In these cases, a bar chart, or even a doughnut chart, may serve your needs better.

Creating a PivotChart

The chart types discussed elsewhere in this book are ideally suited for summarizing different types of data. Pie charts display how much a series of categories contribute to a whole, column and bar charts highlight relative values, and line charts indicate how a value changes over time.

What each of these chart types has in common is that they display data from a static source, such as a data list or a table. A line chart, for example, displays data sets with a time category on the horizontal axis and values on the vertical axis. If the data source contains other columns of data that can't be summarized effectively in a line chart, you would have to create an entirely new chart to summarize that other data. Creating multiple charts keeps your data separate, but it also adds bulk to your workbook and can become confusing as you move between worksheets and chart sheets to find the summary you're looking for.

Enter the PivotChart. A PivotChart, which you create based on data contained in a PivotTable, allows you to dynamically rearrange the data in the PivotTable. You can add and remove fields from the chart's data source, change the fields' priority order, alter the fields' placement in the chart, and filter each field's data to narrow down the data displayed in the chart so that you make exactly the point you want to make (such as in Figure 12-1).

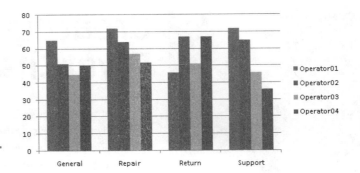

Figure 12-1   A PivotChart
summarizing call data

Using Pivot Data to Create Any Chart You Need

Creating a PivotChart involves formatting your data as a table, generating a PivotTable from the table's data, and then creating a PivotChart. It's essential that you format your worksheet data properly so that you create a usable table, but it's not that difficult to do. After you define your table, creating and populating a PivotTable and PivotChart takes just a few more mouse clicks.

Formatting Data for Use in a PivotChart

Creating a table (which Microsoft formally refers to as an Excel Table) requires that you define your data as a data list. Data lists have the following characteristics:

- Column headers to provide titles for each of the table's columns

- No blank rows within the body of the table

- A blank column (or the edge of the worksheet) to the left and right of the list data

- A blank row below the last row of data

MEMO

When you create a table in Excel 2007, the table style you click doesn't replace any existing text or cell formatting. For example, if one cell has a yellow background color, applying a table style won't get rid of the yellow, even though that color might clash with the rest of the table. To have the table style's design override any existing formatting, right-click the table style, and then click Apply and Clear Formatting.

In previous versions, you created a data list by formatting the list's column headers so that they stood out from the data in the list. One common formatting style was to make the headers bold and centered within their cells. You don't have to format your column headers differently when you create a table in Excel 2007; instead, in the Format as Table dialog (which appears when you click the desired table style), select the My Table Has Headers check box to have Excel treat the first row in your data list as the column headers. Your table will look like the example shown in Figure 12-2.

To create the table shown in Figure 12-2, you select any cell in a data list, click a table style, verify that Excel will include the desired cell range in your table, indicate that your data list contains column headers, and create the table.

Operator	Hour	Calls
Operator01	9:00 AM	10
Operator01	10:00 AM	11
Operator01	11:00 AM	14
Operator01	12:00 PM	5
Operator01	1:00 PM	20
Operator01	2:00 PM	20
Operator01	3:00 PM	8
Operator01	4:00 PM	12
Operator01	5:00 PM	18
Operator02	9:00 AM	15
Operator02	10:00 AM	10
Operator02	11:00 AM	12
Operator02	12:00 PM	6
Operator02	1:00 PM	9
Operator02	2:00 PM	17
Operator02	3:00 PM	18
Operator02	4:00 PM	20
Operator02	5:00 PM	11
Operator03	9:00 AM	15
Operator03	10:00 AM	6
Operator03	11:00 AM	19
Operator03	12:00 PM	6
Operator03	1:00 PM	17
Operator03	2:00 PM	5
Operator03	3:00 PM	14

Figure 12-2 An Excel 2007 table

1. Open the Excel 2007 file Chap12CallTable.xlsx. The first page of data contains a table that lists one week's hourly call volumes for a fictitious company.

2. Select any cell that contains data, click Home | Format as Table, and then click the table style you want to apply.

3. In the Format as Table dialog, verify that the data range $B$2:$D$38 appears in the Where Is the Data for Your Table field and that the My Table Has Headers check box is selected, and then click OK.

Creating a PivotTable and PivotChart

Once you have created a table, you can create a PivotTable and PivotChart using the table as the data source. Tables are ideally suited to serve as PivotTable data sources, so the process takes just a few steps. After you create the PivotTable and PivotChart, you can define their configurations by dragging the PivotTable field headers to the desired locations in the PivotTable Field List task pane (the results of which appear in Figure 12-3).

THE EASY WAY

Prior to Excel 2007, it took several steps to update a PivotTable and PivotChart to reflect new rows in the source data list. When you create a PivotTable using a table as its source, you can click any cell in the PivotTable and then click PivotTable Tools | Options | Refresh to include the new data in the PivotTable and PivotChart summary.

To create the PivotChart shown in Figure 12-3, you will identify the table that contains the data to be summarized and then insert a PivotTable and PivotChart into a new worksheet.

1. Open the Excel 2007 file Chap12CallsForPivot.xlsx. The first page of data contains an Excel Table that lists two years of monthly call volumes for a fictitious company.

2. Select any cell that contains data, and click Insert | PivotTable | PivotChart. Because the data is a table, Excel will guess that the table contains the data to be summarized. Excel then displays the Create PivotTable and PivotChart dialog.

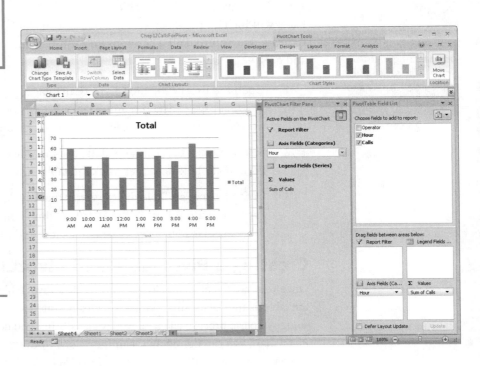

Figure 12-3   Use the PivotTable Field List task pane to organize your PivotChart data.

3. Verify that the Calls table appears in the Table/Range field of the dialog and that the New Worksheet option is selected, and then click OK.

4. In the PivotTable Field List task pane, drag the Hour field header to the Axis Fields (Categories) area, and drag the Calls field header to the Values area.

When you created the PivotChart, four new tabs appeared on the ribbon: Design, Layout, Format, and Analyze. The following list details the capabilities enabled by each of the tabs.

- **PivotChart Tools | Design**   This tab allows you to change the basic colors and design of the PivotChart. The buttons on this tab also enable you to change the PivotChart's chart type, change the data displayed in the PivotChart, select a new color scheme for the PivotChart, and change the basic layout of the PivotChart.

- **PivotChart Tools | Layout**   This tab allows you to fine-tune the layout of your PivotChart. You can hide or display the PivotChart's elements (axes, gridlines, legend, and so on), add pictures or shapes to the PivotChart to help viewers interpret the PivotChart's data, and add a trend line to see what your data will look like in the future if the current trend continues. You can also change the formatting of any part of the PivotChart by selecting it from the drop-down list in the Current Selection group at the far left side of the ribbon.

- **PivotChart Tools | Format**   This tab lets you change the appearance of the fills, lines, and effects for the PivotChart, as well as the appearance of any text in the PivotChart.

- **PivotChart Tools | Analyze**   This tab enables you to hide or display the PivotChart Filter Pane and the PivotTable Field List task pane, refresh the PivotChart's connection to its data source, clear any formats or filters applied to the PivotChart, and change how the PivotChart data is organized.

THE EASY WAY

If you create a PivotTable and later decide you want to create a PivotChart to go along with it, click any cell in the PivotTable and then use the ribbon controls on the Insert tab to create a new chart. Excel recognizes that you used a PivotTable as the data source, so it creates a PivotChart instead of a regular chart.

The default formatting Excel applies to a PivotChart presents your data in a highly usable and understandable manner. Of course, refining the appearance and composition of your PivotChart using the tools available on the Design, Layout, Format, and Analyze tabs enables you to match your organization's preferred styles and color scheme while presenting your data most effectively.

Changing the Data That Shows in Your PivotChart

PivotCharts summarize data stored in PivotTables, but you might not need to summarize all of the data in support of a particular analysis. For example, you might only want to display the calls your technical support line received on Mondays and Fridays in January, which are usually the busiest days of the week during the busiest support month of the year.

Excel 2007 enables you to create two kinds of filters: selection filters, which limit the data shown in a PivotChart to those items you select (e.g., the days Monday and Friday), and rule filters, where you define a rule by which Excel limits the data (e.g., only summarize the data for days where there were more than 100 calls).

Filtering a PivotChart by Rule

As the name implies, rule filters restrict the data summarized in a PivotChart by applying one or more criteria to decide which rows from the PivotTable to include in the PivotChart. You create a rule filter by clicking the down arrow to the right of a field header in the PivotChart Filter Pane or the PivotTable Field List task pane, clicking Value Filters, and then selecting the type of rule you want to create.

After you fill in the filter criteria and click OK, Excel redraws your PivotChart to reflect the new data set (as shown in Figure 12-4).

To create the PivotChart shown in Figure 12-4, you will define a filter that limits the data displayed in the PivotChart to the number of customer service calls completed from 11:00 A.M. to 1:59 P.M. (that is, during the hours between 11:00 A.M. and 1:00 P.M., inclusive).

MEMO

The filter options that appear when you click a filter arrow in a PivotTable or one of the down arrows in the PivotChart Filter Pane change to reflect the type of data in the field. If the field contains a mix of data types, Excel displays the Number Filters menu item.

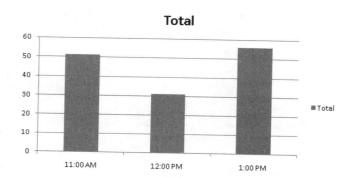

Figure 12-4   Filtering a PivotChart limits the data summarized by the chart.

1. Open the Excel 2007 file Chap12CallsByHour.xlsx. The CVSummary worksheet contains a PivotChart that summarizes one day's hourly call volumes for four operators at a fictitious company.

2. If necessary, select the PivotChart to display the PivotChart Filter Pane.

3. In the PivotChart Filter Pane, click the Axis Fields (Categories) box's down arrow, point to Date Filters, and then click Between to display the Date Filter (Hour) dialog.

4. Verify that the operator "is between" appears in the left-hand box, type **11:00 AM** in the center box, and then type **1:00 PM** in the right-hand box. Click OK when you're done.

After you click OK, the PivotChart changes to display just the hourly call volumes for the hours starting from 11:00 A.M. to 1:00 P.M.

Filtering a PivotChart by Selection

Not every filter lends itself to a rule expressed in terms of values less than or greater than some other value, the first three months of the year, or sales representatives whose names begin with the letter "S." For those cases where you want to display data for categories where the categories don't follow a set rule, you can select the items you do want to display. When you click a filter arrow, Excel displays a list of the values in the PivotTable field. You can use the list to select which values you want to summarize, greatly simplifying a complex PivotChart into the much more easily understood example shown in Figure 12-5.

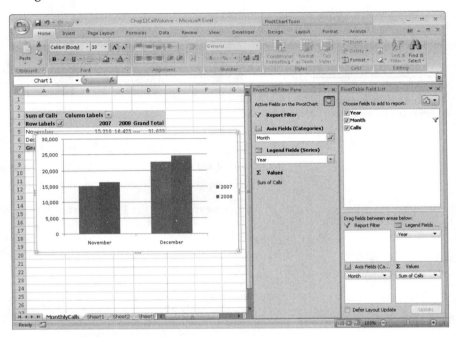

162

Figure 12-5 Pick which values you want to summarize in your PivotChart.

To create the PivotChart shown in Figure 12-5, you will define a selection filter that limits the data displayed in the PivotChart to the number of customer service calls received in November and December of the two years summarized in the data set.

1. Open the Excel 2007 file Chap12CallVolume.xlsx. The MonthlyCalls worksheet contains a PivotChart that summarizes two years' monthly call volumes for a fictitious company.

2. If necessary, select the PivotChart to display the PivotChart Filter Pane.

3. In the PivotChart filter pane, click the Axis Fields (Categories) box's down arrow to display a menu of sorting and filtering options. Click Select All to clear the check boxes in the filter pane, select the November and December check boxes, and then click OK.

After you click OK, the PivotChart changes to display just the hourly call volumes for November and December.

Assigning Fields to the Report Filter Area

PivotCharts enable you to summarize large volumes of data effectively, but you must manage that power and flexibility to ensure your charts remain understandable. It's easy to create PivotCharts that contain enough subdivisions to make the chart more confusing than informative.

Rather than attempt to fit all of those subdivisions into a single chart, you can add fields to the Report Filter area of the PivotChart. Fields in the Report Filter area limit the data summarized in the chart without affecting the chart's organization. As in the case of the PivotChart shown in Figure 12-6, you could move the Category field to the Report Filter area and use that field to limit the data shown in your PivotChart.

To create the PivotChart shown in Figure 12-6, you are going to create a filter that limits the data displayed in the PivotChart to the number of customer service calls relating to returns and repairs received during one business week.

1. Open the Excel 2007 file Chap12CallsByCategory.xlsx. The CVByCategory worksheet contains a PivotChart that summarizes five days' worth of call volumes, broken down by the reason for the call, for four operators at a fictitious company.

2. If necessary, select the PivotChart to display the PivotChart Filter Pane.

3. In the PivotChart Filter Pane, click the Report Filter box's down arrow, and then select the Select Multiple Items check box.

4. In the list of items, clear the General and Support check boxes, and then click OK.

THE EASY WAY

If your PivotTable and PivotChart draw their data from an external source, such as a database stored on another computer, you might find that it takes a long time for the PivotTable to update after you reconfigure its fields. You can avoid most of these delays by selecting the Defer Layout Update check box at the bottom of the PivotTable Field List task pane before you make the adjustments. When you're done making your changes, click the Update button to have Excel update your PivotTable and PivotChart. Be sure to uncheck the Defer Layout Update check box if you want Excel to update your PivotTable whenever you change its fields' arrangement.

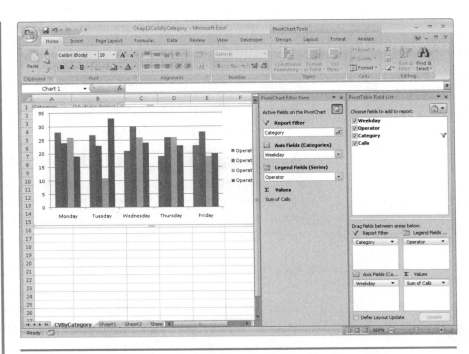

Figure 12-6 Fields in the Report Filter area don't affect the PivotChart's organization.

Changing What You See by Changing the PivotTable

PivotCharts draw their data from PivotTables. While you can create filters to limit the data that appears in a PivotChart, you can't rearrange the fields of the PivotTable to change the organization of the data from within the PivotChart. You can, however, change the appearance of the PivotChart by rearranging the fields in the PivotTable. The results of one such operation appear in Figure 12-7.

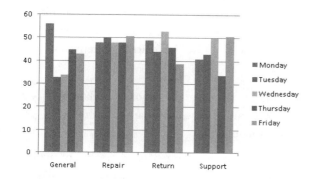

Figure 12-7 Changing the organization of a PivotTable changes how data is displayed in your PivotChart.

To create the PivotTable and PivotChart shown in Figure 12-7, you will swap the positions of the Weekday and Category fields to change the PivotTable organization.

1. Open the Excel 2007 file Chap12CallsPivotTable.xlsx. The CVByCategory worksheet contains a PivotChart that summarizes five days' worth of call volumes, broken down by the reason for the call, for four operators at a fictitious company.

2. If necessary, select the PivotChart to display the PivotTable Field List task pane.

3. In the PivotTable Field List task pane, drag the Category field header from the Legend Fields area to the Axis Fields area. The PivotTable changes to reflect the new arrangement.

4. In the PivotTable Field List task pane, drag the Weekday field from the Axis Fields area to the Legend Fields area.

Finding the Right Chart Type for Your Filtered Data

PivotTables and PivotCharts enable you to reorganize and filter your data on the fly, which means that a single chart type won't always summarize your data effectively. For example, if you organize your PivotTable so that it shows sales for each day of the week, you should select a column or bar chart to compare the relative daily values, or create a pie chart to indicate how much each day's sales contributes to the whole.

The following list summarizes the strengths of the chart types available to you in Excel 2007. Be sure to experiment with your data—you never know when you'll find a combined chart type and PivotTable arrangement that makes a point clearly.

- *Column* charts best summarize the several categories of data. For example, you could use a column chart to compare monthly sales totals for a company's salespeople.

- *Line* charts are most useful for summarizing data where one of the data series is a time component. Rather than comparing every sales representative's totals for a particular month, you could create a line chart that displayed a single representative's monthly sales totals for every month in the current year.

- *Pie* charts best illustrate the contribution each member of a data series makes to the whole. In the sales example, you could find each sales representative's yearly total, and create a pie chart that displays each representative's contribution to the whole.

- *Bar* charts are useful for comparing the relative magnitude of several values. Consider using a bar chart when the category labels are too large to fit on the horizontal axis of your chart.

- *Area* charts illustrate the differences of several sets of data over time. Unlike line charts, which show how individual data series change over time but don't emphasize the relative values in the series, area charts clearly show which values are larger.

- *Scatter* charts let you summarize data sets that have two numerical data series. For example, if your company were testing how price changes affected a product's unit sales, you could plot total revenue for sales at a particular price on the vertical axis, and plot the price points on the horizontal axis.

■ *Stock* charts, as the name implies, are often used to summarize daily stock price fluctuations.

■ *Surface* charts plot three data series and, like a topographic map displays the highest point on a landscape, indicate where the values in two data series combine to generate the largest result. For example, you could create a surface chart that compared how the combination of product price changes and advertising dollars spent in a market affected overall sales revenue in that market.

■ *Doughnut* charts are similar to pie charts in that they visually summarize how much individual values contribute to a whole. Doughnut charts, however, can summarize multiple data series, not just one.

■ *Bubble* charts are like scatter charts, except that the size of the indicator in the body of the charts reflects the magnitude of a third value. For example, if a scatter chart plotted total sales revenue at a price point and the various unit prices, the third value could be the number of units sold at each price.

■ *Radar* charts summarize data contained in a crosstab data table, which is a grid with two categories, such as month and product, and the sales values in the cells where the rows and columns intersect.

What Your PivotChart Can Tell You

PivotTables and PivotCharts enable you to emphasize various aspects of your data, whether by changing how the data is organized within the PivotTable, filtering the data using the controls in the PivotChart Filter Pane, selecting a new chart type with which to summarize your data, or by applying a combination of those techniques.

In the following procedure, you will work through a sequence of PivotChart and PivotTable positions that illustrate a potential business analysis scenario. During that analysis, you will display the total number of calls received over the course of a week, break out those calls by category, change the chart's type to a pie chart to determine how much each category contributed to overall call volume, summarize one operator's calls by category, and further break down that operator's calls by day.

1. Open the Excel 2007 file Chap12CallsAnalysis.xlsx. The Week1Calls worksheet contains a PivotChart that summarizes five days' worth of call volumes, broken down by the reason for the call, for four operators at a fictitious company. The PivotChart will be blank at this point.

2. If necessary, select the PivotChart to display the PivotChart Filter Pane. Then, in the PivotTable Field List task pane, drag the Calls field header from the Choose Fields to Add to Report area to the Values area. The PivotChart displays a single column indicating the total number of calls received during the week.

3. In the PivotTable Field List task pane, drag the Category field header from the Choose Fields to Add to Report area to the Legend Fields area. The PivotChart displays four columns, indicating the total number of calls received for each support category during the week (as shown in Figure 12-8).

4. Click PivotChart Tools | Design | Change Chart Type to display the Change Chart Type dialog. In the left-hand column of that dialog, click the Pie chart type. Verify that the first pie chart subtype is selected, and then click OK. Then, in the PivotTable Field List task pane, drag the Category field header from the Legend Fields area to the Axis Fields area.

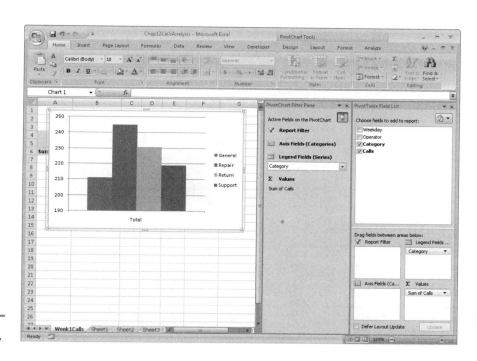

Figure 12-8   A PivotChart
emphasizing calls by category

5. In the PivotTable Field List task pane, drag the Operator field header
   to the Report Filter area. In the PivotChart Filter Pane, click the
   Operator field's down arrow, click Operator03, and then click OK.

6. In the PivotTable Field List task pane, drag the Weekday field header to
   the Report Filter area. In the PivotChart Filter Pane, click the Weekday
   field's down arrow, click Thursday, and then click OK. The results of
   your operation appear in Figure 12-9.

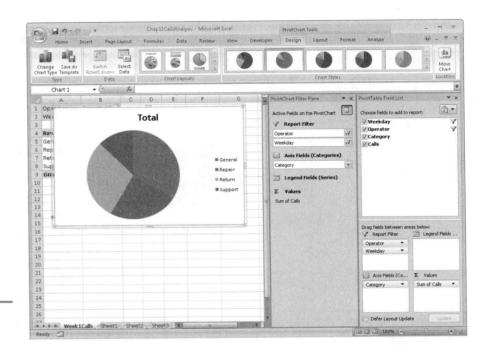

Figure 12-9   A PivotChart filtered by weekday and operator

Every step of this analysis highlighted a different aspect of your data. Be sure to try many PivotTable arrangements and filters to see what you can discover by looking at your data from different perspectives.

Creating Charts for Use in Word and PowerPoint

Each Office 2007 program has its own strengths. Considering only the three Office 2007 programs with the new ribbon user interface, Excel enables you to manage and present financial and scientific data effectively, Word lets you create professional documents and reports, and PowerPoint enables you to present your data attractively and persuasively.

Rather than using each program independently, you can take advantage of all three programs' capabilities by incorporating Excel 2007 charts into Word documents and PowerPoint presentations. Excel charts summarize data succinctly, which adds significant value to your reports, summaries, and briefings. Beyond the information included in the chart, you can add flair to your presentations by adding PowerPoint animations to your chart and its elements.

In this chapter you will learn how to send a chart from an Excel workbook to a Word document (as shown in Figure 13-1) or PowerPoint presentation, create a chart within Word or PowerPoint, and animate charts you have included in a PowerPoint presentation.

Monthly Return Summary

The following table and chart summarize the number of product returns received during the last month, broken out by product.

Category	Calls
Teddy Bear	146
Talking Doll	42
Skateboard	202
Puzzle	435

Returns

- Teddy Bear
- Talking Doll
- Skateboard
- Puzzle

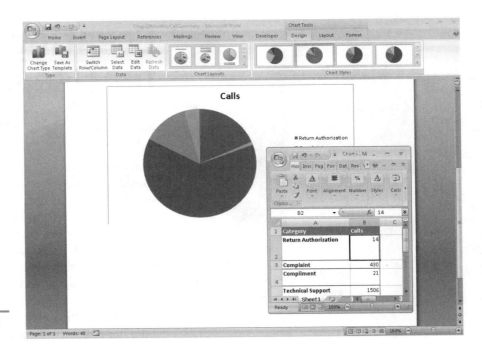

Figure 13-1   Editing a chart
in a Word 2007 document

Sending a Chart from Excel to Word or PowerPoint

Office 2007 programs enable you to move data and objects among different types of documents by using the standard copy-and-paste methods you would use to copy the contents of one worksheet cell to another. When you paste a chart into a Word 2007 document or PowerPoint 2007 presentation, the destination program displays the Paste Options button. If the Paste Options button doesn't appear, press CTRL-Z or click the Undo button on the Quick Access toolbar to undo the paste operation, and then click Office Button | Word Options | Advanced, and then, in the Cut, Copy, and Paste section of the dialog page, select the Show Paste Options Buttons check box.

Click OK to close the Word Options dialog, and paste the chart again; this time, the Paste Options button (shown in Figure 13-2) will appear.

Clicking the Paste Options button displays five options that affect how Excel pastes your chart into the destination. The available options are:

- If you want to paste the chart into your Word 2007 document or PowerPoint presentation and maintain a link to the chart's source data, click *Chart (Linked to Excel Data)*.

- If you want to paste the chart into your document or presentation and allow access to the entire workbook from within the document, click *Excel Chart (Entire Workbook)*.

- If you want to paste the chart as a static image, click *Paste as Picture*.

- If you want to paste the chart in its original format, rather than applying the formatting in the Word document or PowerPoint presentation, click *Keep Source Formatting*.

- If you want to paste the chart and have Word or PowerPoint apply its active theme, click *Use Destination Theme*.

To create the document shown in Figure 13-2, you will

MEMO

If you paste a chart into a Word 97-2003 document or PowerPoint 97-2003 presentation that you opened in Compatibility Mode, Excel 2007 pastes the chart as a static picture and does not display the Paste Options button.

1. Open the Excel 2007 file Chap13ChartToWord.xlsx and the Word 2007 file Chap13MonthlyReturns.docx. The workbook contains a chart summarizing product returns for a fictitious company.

2. In the Chap13ChartToWord.xlsx workbook, on the Chart1 sheet, right-click the chart, and then click Copy.

3. In Chap13MonthlyReturns.docx, click below the existing text, and then click Home | Paste.

4. In Chap13ChartToWord.xlsx, change the value in cell C6 to **43**.

5. Display the Word 2007 document. The chart you pasted into the document reflects the new value in the source table.

173

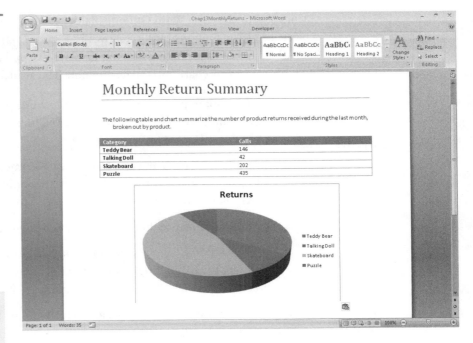

Figure 13-2 Use the Paste Options button to control how you paste your chart into Word or PowerPoint.

MEMO

If you opened a Word 97-2003 document or PowerPoint 97-2003 presentation in Compatibility Mode, you can create a chart from within Word by clicking Insert | Chart, which launches the Microsoft Graph Helper application. You can then edit the chart's data in the datasheet that appears and modify the chart by right-clicking it and clicking the option (such as Chart Type) you want to change.

Creating a Chart in Word or PowerPoint

Instead of opening Excel 2007 as a separate program, creating a chart, and then copying the chart into your document or presentation, you can create an Excel 2007 chart directly in Word 2007 or PowerPoint 2007. To do so, click Insert | Chart and then use the chart tools to modify or format the chart. Charts that you create in Word or PowerPoint will be embedded in that program's file; the chart's source data is stored in an Excel worksheet that is stored as part of the PowerPoint presentation or Word document.

When you click Insert | Chart, Word or PowerPoint embeds an Excel 2007 chart object in the active document, displays the chart, and opens an Excel workbook that contains a table with sample data for the chart. You can then edit the data in the table and resize the table so that it fits your data exactly.

If you already have the data you want to chart in a Word or PowerPoint table or an Excel worksheet, you can select the data, click Home | Copy to copy it, click the upper-left cell in the chart's source table, and click Home | Paste to paste the data into the table. If the data doesn't fit the table exactly, which it probably won't, you can resize the table by clicking any cell in the table and dragging the blue marker at the lower-right corner of the table so that the table contains exactly the data you want to chart. You can clean up the worksheet by deleting any data outside the table and saving your work (your end product might look like the chart displayed in Figure 13-3). To dismiss the Excel workbook, click Office Button | Close or click the Close button at the upper-right corner of the Excel program window.

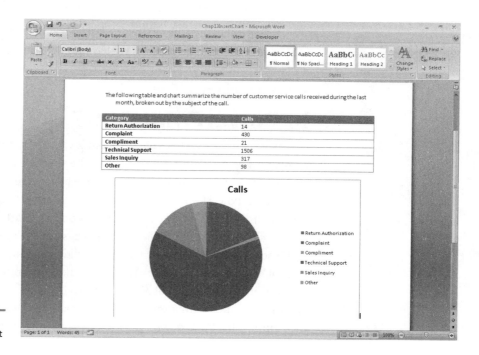

Figure 13-3   A chart created within a Word 2007 document

After you close the source workbook, you can redisplay it at any time by selecting the chart and then clicking Chart Tools | Design | Edit Data.

To create the chart displayed in Figure 13-3, you will insert a chart into a Word 2007 document, copy data from a Word 2007 table into the Excel 2007 workbook that contains the chart's source data, and resize the table to fit the data.

1. Open the Word 2007 file Chap13InsertChart.docx. The document contains a table summarizing customer service calls received by a fictitious company.

2. Click Insert | Chart to display the Insert Chart dialog. Click the Pie category name, and then click OK to accept the default pie chart subtype.

3. Redisplay the Chap13InsertChart.docx file, and copy the data in the table above the chart. Go back to the Chart in Microsoft Office Word workbook, click cell A1, and then click Home | Paste.

4. Redisplay the Chap13InsertChart.docx file to verify that the chart reflects the data you just pasted into the workbook.

Animating Charts in PowerPoint 2007

Charts visually summarize data, enabling viewers to comprehend their company's performance quickly. While the source data is the most important element in any chart, you should also take advantage of the presentation tools available in PowerPoint 2007 to make your points more effectively. One of those tools is the ability to add an animation to a chart.

Like slide animations, which add effects such as fade-ins, diagonal wipes, and blackouts when you move from one slide to another, chart animations control how PowerPoint displays a chart when you move to the slide that contains it. To see the list of animations available for a chart, click the chart, and then, on the Animations tab of the ribbon, in the Animations group, click the Animate list box's down arrow to display the list of available animations.

MEMO

The list of animations changes to reflect the selected chart's type.

When you hover your mouse pointer over an animation that interests you, PowerPoint displays a Live Preview of what that animation will look like. Clicking the animation assigns it to the slide.

After you assign an animation to your chart, you can customize it in many ways. For example, you can change its speed so that it occurs more quickly or more slowly, begin the animation with the background elements (such as the title and legend) already drawn, or delay the start of the animation.

To customize an animation after you assign it to a chart, click the chart and then click Animations | Custom Animation to display the Custom Animation task pane. The Custom Animation task pane, shown in Figure 13-4, displays a list of animations applied to the chart; the order in which the animations will occur; and tools you can use to add, edit, or delete the chart's animations. If you want to edit or delete an existing animation, you can do so by clicking the animation in the list and using the controls in the task pane.

Figure 13-4 The Custom Animation task pane's tools give you control over your chart's animations.

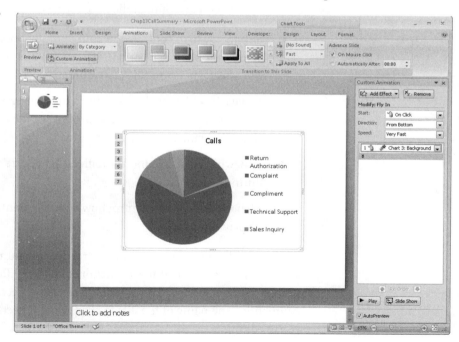

MEMO

Be careful not to use the controls in the Animation tab's Transition to This Slide group on the ribbon when you want to create chart animations. The Transition to This Slide group's controls affect the slide as a whole, not the chart.

When you select an animation, you can use the three controls in the Modify section of the Custom Animation task pane to change the animation. The top control, Start, lets you control when the animation begins. The bottom control, Speed, lets you vary how quickly or slowly the animation occurs. The middle control changes to reflect the type of animation you selected.

Clicking the Start controls enables you to select whether an animation element occurs when you click the mouse (or, during a slide show, press the SPACEBAR, PAGE DOWN, or PAGE UP button, or the N or P keys), happens at the same time as the previous animation element, or happens automatically after the previous animation element (what theatrical lighting technicians call an *autofollow* cue). The Speed list box contains five settings: Very Fast (0.5 seconds), Fast (1 second), Medium (2 seconds), Slow (3 seconds), and Very Slow (5 seconds).

Selecting an animation from the list and then clicking the Change button enables you to edit any of the following four elements of the animation:

- *Entrance,* which controls the animation that occurs when you first display the slide that contains the chart (this is the animation element you affect when you select an animation from the Animate list box)

- *Emphasis,* which enables you to change the size of the chart elements; the size, font, and font style of any text in the chart; and whether the chart elements spin as they are added

- *Exit,* which controls the animation that occurs when you leave the slide during a slide show

- *Motion paths,* which control how chart elements move when you display the slide

If you'd like more fine-grained control over an animation, click the down arrow at the right edge of the animation, and click Effect Options to display a dialog (shown in Figure 13-5) with three tabs: Effect, Timing, and Chart Animation. The name of the dialog changes to reflect the type of animation you're editing.

Figure 13-5   Clicking Effect Options unveils more ways to control your chart animations.

The controls on the Effect page of the dialog let you change the effect's settings, add a sound if desired, control whether (and how) to dim the item after it is animated, and animate any text in the selected element. The controls on the Timing page let you select when the animation starts (as mentioned earlier in this section), add a delay before the animation starts, change the animation's speed, have the animation repeat one or more times, and have PowerPoint play the animation backwards (rewind) after it finishes. The Chart Animation tab's controls let you select whether to affect the chart element by element and whether to start the animation with the chart's background (usually the legend, title, and axes titles) already drawn.

When you're ready to test the animation, you can do so by clicking the Play button at the bottom of the Custom Animation task pane (as shown in Figure 13-6).

To create the animation displayed in Figure 13-6, you will create a fly-in animation, change the animation's speed, and then edit the animation so that it begins with the chart's background already drawn.

1. Open the PowerPoint 2007 file Chap13CallSummary.docx. The presentation contains a chart summarizing customer service calls received by a fictitious company.

2. On the Animation tab of the ribbon, in the Animations group, click the Animate list box's down arrow, and then, in the Fly In group on the menu, click By Category.

3. Click Animations | Custom Animation to display the Custom Animation task pane. In the Modify section of the task pane, click the Speed list box's down arrow, and then click Fast.

MEMO

By default, PowerPoint previews the animation when you create it. If you don't want to wait for your animation sequence to run, uncheck the AutoPreview check box at the bottom of the Custom Animation task pane.

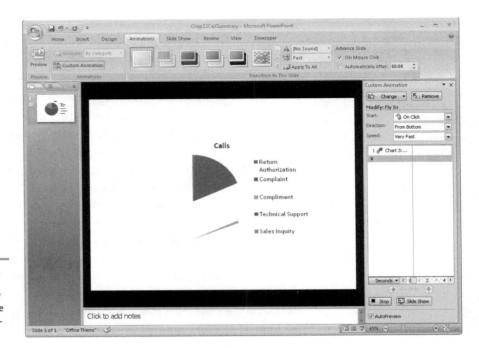

Figure 13-6 To see what your animation will look like in a slide show, click the Play button (which changes to the Stop button while the animation runs).

4. In the list of animations applied to the chart (there should be just one), click the animation's down arrow, and click Effect Options. In the Fly In dialog, click the Chart Animation tab, uncheck the Start Animation by Drawing the Chart Background check box, and click OK.

5. In the Custom Automation task pane, click the Play button to play the animation.

Printing Charts

Now that you have the chart you want and it looks exactly how you want it to look, you're ready to print it out. In this chapter, though, to "print" doesn't only mean sending the chart to the printer. You can also create a Portable Document Format (PDF) file or save it so that you can publish it on the Web.

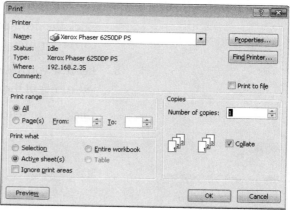

Printing a Chart Using a Physical Printer

This is the simplest way to print your chart, and one you're likely used to.

1. Decide if you want to print the chart alone or both the chart and the data used to create it.

2. If you want to print the chart only, select it in the worksheet.

3. Click the Office Button or press CTRL-P. A dialog like the one in Figure 14-1 will appear.

4. Click the drop-down menu under Printer | Name to select the correct printer.

5. Because you've selected the chart, the Print What section in the lower-left corner of the dialog should have the Active sheet(s) option selected.

6. Click OK to send the print job.

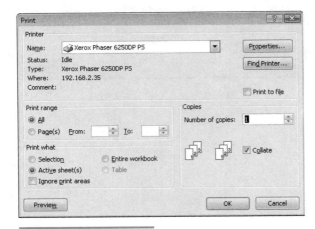

Figure 14-1 Print dialog

If you want to print the chart and the data in the worksheet:

1. Create the chart in the worksheet, or copy and paste it from the worksheet/document/presentation in which it is located.

2. Click the chart's border (not a corner and not in the middle of any side), and drag it to where you want it.

3. To adjust the chart's size, click the chart and then click Format | Size. Enter the desired height and width values to size the chart to your liking.

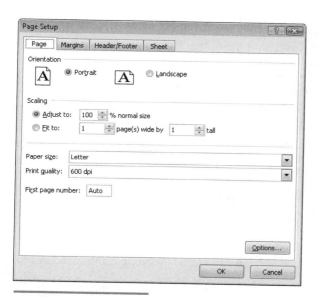

Figure 14-2   Page Setup dialog

To see how the print job will look, click the Office Button in the upper-left corner and then click Print | Print Preview.

- If the chart doesn't look good in the default setting, would changing the page's orientation work? Click Page Layout | Orientation to see if Portrait or Landscape orientation works better.

- If your chart is exactly as small as it can be and stay legible but doesn't quite fit on the page, adjusting the margins slightly might solve your problem. You can do this by going to Page Layout | Margins and either choosing one of the available options or Custom Margins, which will give you the Page Setup dialog shown in Figure 14-2.

- If that still doesn't work, you may need to increase the size of the paper you're using to print. To change the paper size, go to Page Layout | Size, and select the one you want. The other two paper sizes used (in the U.S.) are 11" x 14" (legal) and 11" x 17" (tabloid).

Printing a Chart to an Adobe .pdf or a Microsoft .xps File

If you don't need to print the chart, or if you want to put it in a file so that it is a picture instead of an editable format, you can, if your system configuration allows you do it, "print" your document into a PDF or XMS Paper Specification (XPS) file. It's a simple process.

1. Click the Office logo, and select Print.

MEMO

If you don't have the ability to save or print in either of these formats, you need to install the add-in, which can be downloaded by machines with validated copies of Office from www .microsoft.com. Press F1 or click the question mark in the upper-right corner of Excel to access Microsoft Office Help. A suggested search string is "save as PDF," which will lead you to an entry giving you the download link from an overly long Uniform Resource Locator (URL).

2. When the Print dialog appears (as seen in Figure 14-1), click the drop-down menu to see if you have the option to save your document in either of these formats.

3. By clicking Print, instead of sending the chart to a printer, your system will take you through the process of saving your document in a file in the new format. If you don't have the option to print to PDF or XPS, see if you can use the Save As dialog to do the same thing.

Preparing Your Chart for Web Publishing

But what if you need to share your chart with your co-workers over the Web? This is a great way to maintain version control, as everyone can have access to the chart, but it will only be changed when the original workbook is changed, and that's only if you set it up so that the chart is updated when the workbook is changed.

Making Your Chart a Web Document

The first step in this process is to convert your chart from an Excel file into one that's web-publishable. For this example, I'll use the Gold Optimal Versus Actual worksheet from the Chap9Table.xlsx file.

1. Open the file Chap9Table.xlsx and go to the Gold Optimal Versus Actual worksheet.

2. Select cells A1 through C3.

3. Select Insert | Charts | Other Charts | Doughnut to create your chart.

4. Click Office Button | Save As | Other Formats to display the Save As dialog. Click the Save as Type list box's down arrow, and select Web Page. After doing so, you will see a dialog like the one in Figure 14-3.

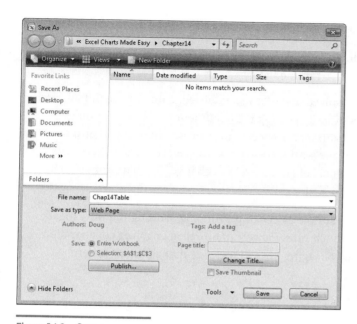

Figure 14-3   Save as
Web Page dialog

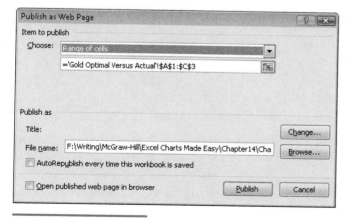

Figure 14-4   Publish as
Web Page dialog

5. Choose if you want to publish the
    entire workbook or only the sheet you
    are working with.

6. Give the page a title if you wish to
    do so.

7. Click Publish. You will see a dialog like
    the one in Figure 14-4.

8. If you wish to publish the entire
    workbook, you can do so by selecting
    Choose | Entire Workbook. You
    also have the option of publishing
    previously published items, a range of
    cells, or any other worksheet in the file.

9. If you want to give the page a title,
    click the Change button to the right
    of the dialog.

10. Below the filename line is a check box,
    giving you the option to autorepublish
    every time the workbook is saved. That
    way, if the workbook, the authoritative
    source for the page's content, is
    changed, it will automatically be
    reflected on the published web page.

11. To verify that your web page was
    created successfully, click the Start
    button in the lower-left corner of your
    screen, and select Recent Items.

12. Select your web-published file. Your
    page will open in Internet Explorer.

FAQ

FAQ: I don't want to lose version control on my workbook, but I need to give people access to my chart immediately!

Answer: This can be solved if you have a knowledge management tool, such as Microsoft SharePoint. By posting the document to the portal, you will enable all those with at least read access to see your chart. If you post the entire workbook, anyone with read-write privileges will be able to modify the data in your spreadsheet and, therefore, change the chart immediately if Autorepublish is enabled.

Printing can be as simple as clicking Print and sending the worksheet to the printer. Excel is much more powerful, however, enabling collaboration with any authorized colleagues via a knowledge management system.

Index

193

195